Physical Characteristics of the Sloughi

(from the United Kennel Club breed standard)

Body: A properly proportioned Sloughi is squarish to slightly higher than long.

Tail: Long, thin and set in line with the croup, carried low with a typical upward curve in the resting position. The tail should be long enough to reach the point of the hocks.

Hindquarters: Lean, flat and muscular. The second thigh is long and well muscled. Hocks are strong and well bent. The rear pasterns are strong and have no dewclaws. The hindlegs are moderately angulated.

Color: The coat colors of the Sloughi are all shades of light sand (cream) to mahogany red fawn, with or without black markings such as brindling, black mask, black ears, dark overlay and black mantle, with no invasive white markings.

Height and Weight: For mature males, height at the withers ranges between 26.4–28.3 inches (66–72 cm), with the ideal size being 27.6 inches (70 cm). Weight ranges between 55 and 65 pounds. For mature females, height at the withers ranges between 24–26.7 inches (61–68 cm), with the ideal size being 25.6 inches (65 cm). Weight ranges between 45 and 50 pounds.

Feet: Lean and have the shape of an elongated oval. The nails are black or just pigmented.

Sloughi

◇

By Marie-Dominique
Crapon de Caprona, Ph.D.

Contents

9

History of the Sloughi

Take an in-depth look at the origins of this enchanting rare sighthound from northern Africa. Included are discussions of the breed's people, the Berbers, and the four countries responsible for the breed's origin. Discover how tradition influenced the breed and how it spread outside its homeland. Meet important people and dogs in the establishment of the breed, and compare the Sloughi to other sighthound breeds.

46

Characteristics of the Sloughi

With the distinction of being one of few guarding sighthound breeds, the Sloughi is prized for its keen sighthound instincts, intelligence and noble bearing. Learn the particular requirements of owning a Sloughi to see if the two of you are a good match. Topics include the Sloughi's looks and personality, the breed's innate skills and abilities, considerations for the potential owner and breed-specific health concerns.

58

Breed Standard for the Sloughi

Learn the requirements of a well-bred Sloughi by studying the description of the breed set forth in the United Kennel Club standard. Typical specimens of the breed must possess key characteristics as outlined in the breed standard.

72

Your Puppy Sloughi

Find out about how to locate a well-bred Sloughi puppy. Discover which questions to ask the breeder and what to expect when visiting the litter. Prepare in advance for your puppy's arrival. Also discussed are home safety, the first trip to the vet, helping pup acclimate to his new home and socialization.

90

Proper Care of Your Sloughi

Cover the specifics of taking care of your Sloughi every day: feeding for all stages of life; grooming, including coat care, ears, eyes, nails and bathing; and exercise needs for your dog. Also discussed are the essentials of dog identification.

Contents

Training Your Sloughi   100

Begin with the basics of training the puppy and adult dog. Learn the principles of house-training the Sloughi, including the use of crates and basic scent instincts. Enter Puppy Kindergarten and introduce the pup to his collar and leash and progress to the basic commands. Find out about obedience classes and other activities.

Healthcare of Your Sloughi   119

By Lowell Ackerman DVM, DACVD
Become your dog's healthcare advocate and a well-educated canine keeper. Select a skilled and able veterinarian. Discuss pet insurance, vaccinations and infectious diseases, the neuter/spay decision and a sensible, effective plan for parasite control, including fleas, ticks and worms.

Showing Your Sloughi   144

Step into the center ring and find out about the world of showing pure-bred dogs. Here's how to get started in shows, how they are organized and basic ring procedure. Take a leap into the realms of obedience trials, agility, tracking tests and lure coursing.

Index 156

KENNEL CLUB BOOKS: **SLOUGHI**
ISBN: 1-59378-395-7

Copyright © 2004 • Kennel Club Books, LLC
308 Main Street, Allenhurst, NJ 07711 USA
Cover Design Patented: US 6,435,559 B2 • Printed in South Korea

Photographs by Paulette Braun, T.J. Calhoun, Carolina Biological Supply, Juliette Cunliffe, Dominique de Caprona, Fleabusters Rx for Fleas, Isabelle Français, Daniel Gauss/Shot On Site, Jenny Hatten, Carol Ann Johnson, Bill Jonas, Dr. Dennis Kunkel, Jodi Lewis, Jack McGuffin, Tam C. Nguyen, Phototake, Frank Powers, Jean Claude Revy, Dr. Sabine Schlenkrich, Alex Smith, Kent Standerford and Alice van Kempen.

Illustrations by Dominique de Caprona and Patricia Peters.

The publisher wishes to thank all of the owners of the dogs featured in this book, including Dominique de Caprona, Michal Dubrovsky, Maria Goodman, Michel and Laurence Gouzy, Edith Lehrman, Pam Marston-Pollock, the Newman family, Kate Rodarty and Mrs. F. Stacul.

The Sloughi's history is lost in the desert's sands and extends back thousands of years to ancient Egypt and North Africa. The breed today remains largely unchanged from its original form.

HISTORY OF THE

SLOUGHI

"A pure-bred Sloughi neither eats nor drinks from a dirty vessel; he refuses milk into which someone has plunged his hands. Has he not been trained for delicate disdain? Whereas the common dog, useful and vigilant guardian, is at the most allowed to seek his food among carrion and old bones, whereas he is shamefully repulsed far from the tent and the table, the Sloughi, he, himself, lies in the room reserved for the men, on the carpets at his master's side or even on his bed... He is clothed, protected from the cold with blankets like the horse; it is well known that he is very sensitive to the cold. It is one more proof of his being pure-bred. The Sloughi accompanies his master on his visits; like him he is given hospitality and has his share of each dish. A pure-bred Sloughi never hunts but with his master. He knows by his cleanliness, his respect for conventions, and the graciousness of his manners, how to acknowledge the consideration of which he is the object.... The death of a Sloughi is a cause for mourning for all the tent; women and children weep for him as for a member of the family."

This description from the mid-1800s, the first known portrait of the magnificent Sloughi breed and its role in North African societies, reached us through the well-known books of Général Daumas. These stories were soon to be followed by those of others who had traveled to the North African countries of Morocco, Algeria, Tunisia and Libya. Others stationed there also offered accounts, including Charles Cornevin and particularly Pierre Mégnin (1897). Several enthusiastic accounts about the hunting ability and the temperament of the Sloughi date from the time that France occupied Algeria, and from Dutch traveler Auguste Le Gras (1912) and German traveler Waizenegger (1932–36). According to Durel (1942), it is among the Great Nomadic tribes of the Sahara that the best Sloughis were found. He cites Captain Coget, expert on the Sloughi in its original environment, who said that the best Sloughis were found particularly in the Algerian Moroccan South among the tribes of Oulad Sidi-Cheikh, Oulad-Djerir, Beni-Guil, Oulad Nacer, Doui-Menia and others.

France and Holland were the first to import this breed at the turn of the 20th century. In Holland, Auguste Le Gras brought back five Sloughis, which became the foundation of Dutch Sloughi breeding before World War II. In France, several Sloughis came from Algeria, where the military was stationed, from Tunisia and later from Morocco.

World War II effectively interrupted dog breeding in France, Holland and Germany, and one had to wait for the 1960s to see a renewal of interest in the breed. The end of the conflict between France and Algeria during the late 1960s enabled the importation of new dogs to Europe, as people returning from Algeria brought their Sloughis back with them. At the same time, by the first half of the 20th century, the Sloughi breed became almost extinct in its countries of origin. Political upheavals had disrupted highly sophisticated breeding by leading families. A new law introduced during French occupation, which prohibited hunting with sighthounds, had resulted in the shooting on sight of these dogs. Epidemic rabies had further decimated the Sloughi population. By the end of the 20th century, the countries of origin were making efforts to protect their Sloughi populations as national patrimony, particularly Algeria, through the *Club du Sloughi d'Alger;* and Morocco,

through the *Club du Sloughi Marocain.* However, the breed is still subject to the harsh conditions prevailing in North Africa and has to survive epidemics of rabies, distemper, parvovirus and various local endemic diseases such as babisia and leishmania, as vaccinations for some of these illnesses are not readily available.

Today, the breed, now well established in various European countries and to some extent in the US, is still not very common, and it is treasured by a relatively small, but dedicated, number of enthusiasts.

EARLY HISTORY

The exact origins of the breed are lost in the desert sands, as they date too far back to be completely known and thus remain speculative. Representations of African sighthound-like dogs go back to the seventh and eighth millennium BC, and artifacts of ancient Egypt show us how valuable prick-eared (Tesem) and lop-eared smooth sighthounds were in those days. The smooth lop-eared sighthounds of ancient Egypt are thought to have originated from Asia (east of Egypt), but they were also part of tributes paid to the pharaohs from Nubia (south of Egypt) and possibly Libya. A mummy of such a dog is kept in the Cairo Museum. Its coat color is pale fawn (which we now call "sand").

The history of the Sloughi is linked to the history of its people, the Berbers, who have lived in North Africa since the earliest recorded time. References to them date from about 3000 BC. For many centuries the Berbers inhabited the coast of North Africa from Egypt to Morocco. Over the centuries, various powers dominated the area starting with the Romans.

In 264 BC, Rome engaged with Carthage in a struggle for the control of the Mediterranean Sea. Carthage (now Tunis) at this time was the foremost maritime power in the world, ruling as absolutely in the central and western Mediterranean as did Rome on the Italian peninsula. It became such a power under the leadership of the great general Hamilcar, Hamilcar's son-in-law Hasdrubal and finally Hamilcar's son Hannibal. The Second Punic War began in 218 BC. Hannibal crossed the Alps with an enormous force, descending on Italy from the north, and defeated the Romans in a series of battles; he then continued to ravage most of southern Italy for years. He was recalled to Africa to face Scipio Africanus, who had invaded Carthage. Scipio decisively defeated Hannibal at Zama in 202 BC, and Carthage was compelled to give up its navy, cede Spain and its Mediterranean islands and pay a huge indemnity. From Syria to Spain, the Mediter-

> **COUNTRIES OF ORIGIN**
> Although the Poodle is often believed to have originated in both Germany and France, most breeds of pure-bred dog derive from single countries. The Sloughi is unique in that it derives from the North African region and several countries rightly can lay claim to being the breed's "country of origin." These countries include Morocco, Algeria, Libya and Tunisia.

ranean was now dominated by Rome.

Then came the Vandals, an ancient Germanic tribe of Jutland (now in Denmark), who achieved their greatest power when Gaiseric became king of the tribe in 428 AD. They moved to North Africa the following year and there defeated the Romans. Gaiseric's sovereignty was recognized by the Roman emperor Valentinian III in 422. The Vandals predominated in what is now Algeria and northern Morocco by 435, and conquered Carthage in 439. The Vandals' power began to decline after Gaiseric's death in 477, and in 534 they were defeated by the Byzantine general Belisarius.

Berbers continued to inhabit the region until the seventh century AD, when the Arabs conquered North Africa and drove many Berber tribes inland to the Atlas Mountains and to areas in

Reproduction of "Return from the Hunt," Thebes, 15th Century BC, from the grave of Rekh-mi-Re. This drawing was done by the author, based on a postcard from the Louvre Museum, Paris, France.

Mummy of a lop-eared hound bitch, found in the Cairo Museum, Egypt. It belonged perhaps to Amenhotep or Horemheb, 18TH dynasty, Valley of the Kings.

A well-known mural painting that depicts a pack of hounds, part of a Nubian tribute to the Pharaohs from Nubia, 15th century BC, decorating the grave of Rekh-mi-Re.

and near the Sahara. Beginning about 1045 and continuing at a decreasing rate for several centuries, Bedouin nomads from central Arabia invaded northern Africa. These invaders took over all suitable grazing land and upset the balanced agricultural and urban civilization that the resident Berbers had achieved. The Bedouin flocks destroyed most of the natural ground cover; by over-grazing, the flocks turned pasture-land into semi-desert.

The Ottoman Empire, under Selim I, destroyed the Mameluke Empire in 1517 and conquered Syria, Palestine, Egypt and Arabia, thus incorporating the heartland of the old Islamic caliphates. The Ottoman Empire reached its peak during the reign of Suleiman the Magnificent. The decline of the Ottoman Empire began late in the reign of Suleiman I and continued until the end of World War I in 1918, when it finally collapsed. It was replaced by the modern Republic of Turkey, founded in 1923 by Mustafa Kemal (later Atatürk) from a portion of the Ottoman Empire.

During all of the centuries, it is difficult to know exactly how the various hunting hounds that probably came with the invaders influenced the hounds of the Berbers, how the hounds of the Berbers influenced the dogs of the invaders and how the hounds of the various invaders influenced each other. The Romans bred the Vertragus sighthound. Hunting scenes on mosaic (in the Tunis Museum) show us that the sight-hounds with which the Romans hunted were sand, red, black and brindle, the same coat colors found today in the Sloughi. Which dogs the Vandals brought with them is unclear. It is probable that the Turks had some of their feath-ered sighthounds with them. In fact, such sighthounds were imported from Egypt to the UK at the turn of the 20th century.

Because of the migration of different peoples in that part of the world over the centuries, we cannot ascertain whether or not these ancient Egyptian drop-eared sighthounds are directly related to the drop-eared smooth sight-hounds we know today. The ancient Egyptian drop-eared

HOW'S YOUR ARABIC?
The words "Slughi" (colloquial Arabic) and "Saluki" (classical Arabic) mean "sighthound" in English. The names "Sloughi" and "Saluki" are European spellings of the Arabic words and were used to name these two different breeds by the Western world. They replace the Arabic way of referring to these breeds as Slughi-mogrebi (Sloughi), and Slughi-shami (feathered Saluki) or Slughi-nedji (smooth Saluki). Similarly, the English Greyhound is named Slughi-inglisi. In Afghanistan, sighthounds are named "Tazi" (which means "Arabian"), and this word is used to refer to Salukis, Afghan Hounds and Steppen Afghan Hounds.

hound does resemble today's Sloughi, smooth Saluki, Azawakh and smooth Afghan Hound, but it is impossible without a genetic study to know whether it was a breed of its own, whether it was identical to any one of these four breeds or whether it was the ancestor of all drop-eared sighthounds. The mummy in Cairo tells us that it was a dog of relatively small size, smaller indeed than all four of the breeds mentioned.

Nevertheless, the reader should understand that, in spite of all of these various invaders across the centuries, recent studies on the mitochondrial DNA of today's Egyptian people reveal that they have the same mitochondrial DNA

Basenji (above) and Rhodesian Ridgeback (below), two of the breeds that, along with the Sloughi and the Azawakh, make up the four breeds native to Africa.

as the ancient Egyptians. This proves that local populations of people, and probably of animals as well, even if there was an occasional mixing of bloodlines, remained genetically stable across thousands of years.

THE SLOUGHI IN ITS COUNTRIES OF ORIGIN

MOROCCO

Although the Sloughi was originally the sighthound of the Berber people, Bedouins also developed a relationship with this breed as they invaded the Berbers' territory. In Morocco, the Sloughis are to be found in the Berber villages, where they are free to roam without bothering either cattle or poultry. The finer-boned, smaller Sloughis are used to hunt hare. The stronger Sloughis, often covered with scars, are set loose against jackals, which attack the goat and sheep herds. The few

---

FOUR SMOOTH AFRICANS

The Sloughi is one of two African sighthound breeds recognized by the Fédération Cynologique Internationale (FCI). Whereas the Sloughi originates from North Africa (Algeria, Morocco, Tunisia and Libya), the Azawakh is to be found in Central Africa (Chad, Niger, Burkina Faso and Mali). Other recognized African breeds are the Rhodesian Ridgeback and the Basenji. These four breeds are all smooth-coated.

Sloughis found around towns are usually kept as cherished pets by the affluent Arabs.

In the 1930s, it seems that in Morocco, in contrast to Algeria, most of the Sloughis were sand-colored (Waizenegger 1933–36). Accounts from people returning from dog shows in Casablanca and Rabat in the 1980s and 1990s tell us that most Sloughis in Morocco are sand with black mask or sand brindle with black mask, and a few are red with black mask or sand with black mantle.

Most of the activities of the *Club du Sloughi Marocain* seem to concentrate on north and central Morocco, around the king's towns of Fes, Marrakech, Meknes and Rabat. Sloughis are found between the regions of Ourzazate and Taroudant, Tiznit and Guelmim. The Princess Ruspoli, who has actively pursued the history, standardization and preservation of the breed in Morocco, used to keep a pack of royal Sloughis. Little is known today about the once-famous and exquisite Sloughis of the south.

The Moroccan Sloughi, as we know it today, is considered to be of the "mountain type," substantial and tall (compared to the more lightly built "desert type"). The dogs exported from this country, or used for breeding there, were sand with black mask and black mantle (Abd des Grimoires de Kerfa in France, G'Zel Ouled Laouichat and

MODERN BREEDING

The Sloughi breed was developed in Europe and the US from dogs imported directly from Tunisia, Libya, Morocco and Algeria. Still today, some breeders continue to import dogs from these countries in order to breed as closely as possible to the original country-of-origin dogs.

Amrah in Morocco), sand brindle (Jnah Douar Oulad in Morocco) or sand with black mask (Mansur in Germany, Atika Bint du Maroc in Holland, Mechra-Bel-Ksiri dogs in Switzerland).

ALGERIA

Most of the French literature on Sloughis originated from this country as a result of the French occupation. Xavier Przezdziecki says, in his 1955 enthusiastic description of the breed, that the preferred coat colors are sand with black mask and brindle, but that others also exist (red, black mantle). It is from these accounts that we know of the two types of Sloughis: the lightly built exquisite Sloughi of the desert and the more strongly built impressive mountain Sloughi. In the country of origin, red brindle dogs that were used for breeding all came from or were suspected to be from Algeria (Ramla in the US, Fautchy, rescue

in France). One early brood bitch in France in the early 1960s, Chéchia Bent Abdul des Barines, was red brindle and had Algerian parents, bred by Xavier Pzezdziecki. Other imports were sand with black mask (Auguste LeGras's Muska and Hoëesj, Quitus in France, Richa in the US and others).

TUNISIA

In his informative description of a gazelle hunt, Auguste Le Gras (1921) says that the Tunisian Sloughis are mostly sand-colored. A trip to Tunisia in 1999 revealed a clear difference between the tall, substantial, mountain-type Sloughis found in the Atlas mountains, north of Tunisia, and the smaller, finer-boned, desert-type Sloughis found on the borders of the Sahara Desert. The Sloughis in Tunisia have some relationship to the Libyan Sloughis and the Algerian Sloughis, as this small country shares borders with both of these countries, and its Sloughis are found in sand, red and brindle in both colors. There are a few sand-colored dogs with black mantles as well. Dogs exported from Tunisia were sand with black mask (Auguste Le Gras's Schaab and Zeïna in Holland, Richa el Djerid in Switzerland, Y'Schrab in France), sand with dark overlay (Bedui in Germany), red sand (Rym Cassandra in the US) or sand light brindle (Tarfa in the US).

LIBYA

According to Mrs. van Duyven-bode, the Libyan Sloughi resembles the Tunisian Sloughi. Apart from the rare brindles, most are sand or pale cream with dark brown eyes and black noses, lips and lines around the eyes; few seem to have black masks. Although pups may have dark masks, they fade as the pups grow up; no adults had black masks. The Libyan Sloughi is apparently very homogenous. The average size for the dogs is 27 inches (68–70 cm) and for bitches 25 inches (63–65 cm). Because of the political situation in Libya after the early 1970s, little is known about the situation of the Libyan Sloughi today. Most of the dogs exported out of Libya were sand-colored (Tagiurie el Sian in the US, Damiela in Holland, Dukal Umm Bersheba's el Abid in Switzerland); one was sand brindle (Rodarty, US).

NORTH AFRICAN TRADITIONS

Général Daumas (1850) relates that, in Algeria, "Pleasure is taken in adorning (the Sloughi), in putting shell collars on him. He is protected against the evil eye by the talismans put on him." The feet of the Sloughi are also dipped

The Afghan Hound is a well-known sighthound. There has been some confusion in various countries over correctly distinguishing between the different, lop-eared sighthound breeds.

in henna to bring good luck. In Algeria, at the age of three months, the frein of the tongue (*chaiata* in Arabic) is sometimes cut to give the Sloughi more stamina when racing. In both Algeria and Tunisia, the ears of the Sloughi are cropped up, allegedly to prevent them from being torn to pieces when hunting jackals. A cornered jackal throws himself on his back and defends himself by thrashing with his front paws. The Sloughi's front legs are also branded when the dog is six months old by using a heated "cerpette" applied in a slanted position on the inside of the front leg. Not only are such brands specific for each tribe, they are also thought to keep the dog's legs straight, preventing malformation of the joints, thus improving running. However, the few pictures of Libyan Sloughis show neither cropped-up ears nor any marks on the dogs' front legs. This tradition does not seem to be widespread in Morocco either.

Général Daumas writes that the Sloughi is the only dog treated as family and allowed inside the tent. A Bedouin would go without his own blanket to provide his Sloughi with warmth in the cold desert nights, and puppies were often breast-fed by Bedouin women to help nursing bitches. At the end of his owner's life, the Sloughi is, like the horse, part of the precious inheritance that his owner leaves behind. At the end of the dog's life, the Sloughi is mourned.

Sloughi fancier Armin Schmid met an old Patriarche at the Casablanca dog show in 1989, who told him, *"Quand on rêve d'un Sloughi, on rêve d'un ami"* ("When you dream of a Sloughi, you dream of a friend"). This charming maxim shows the special relationship of the Arab to his Sloughi. Like precious companion dogs from the Orient, a top-quality Sloughi is never sold, but is given as a precious gift to the best of friends.

According to Durel (Algeria, 1942), the Arab takes the breeding of his Sloughis very seriously. The owner of a great dam will ride on horse or mehari (camel) for miles across the desert to take her to a sire who is well known for his beauty and hunting ability. The Arabs have powerful traditions regarding the selection and breeding of Sloughis, thus preserving this fascinating breed to the point that it has become the true incarnation of the gazehound.

A sophisticated Sloughi breeding existed also in Morocco in the 1920s and 1930s. In this country, the secret of breeding Sloughis is passed down from father to son. Such families have had Sloughis for many generations. El Glaoui, the Pasha of Marrakesh and many princesses also have contributed to the high quality of the Moroccan Sloughis.

As Général Daumas tells us: "Only the Sloughi has the esteem, the consideration, the watchful tenderness of his master. That is because the rich, as well as the poor, regard him as a companion of their chivalrous pastimes in which they take such pleasure. For the poor, the Sloughi is also the purveyor who keeps him alive. Thus he is not trained with hurried pains. His breeding is supervised with the same precautions as that of the mare. In the Sahara a man will travel from 25 to 30 leagues to mate a beautiful bitch with a renowned dog capable of taking a gazelle on the run. If by some fatal chance, a bitch (sloughia) has mated with a watchdog, she is made to abort by massaging the young in her belly when they are formed, or else the young are cast off as soon as they have seen the light of day…"

THE SLOUGHI ON THE CONTINENT

We've mentioned that France and Holland were the first to import this breed at the turn of the 20th century. The breed became more well known in Europe in the late 1960s, at the end of the war between France and Algeria, as people returning from Algeria brought their Sloughis with them. Today the Sloughi is bred, exhibited in shows and seen participating in sporting events such as

An example of the rare shorthaired Saluki.

TRIBAL RELATIONS

The Sloughi was originally bred by the Berbers in western North Africa, the Azawakh by the Touaregs (a Berber tribe) in northern central Africa and the Saluki by the Bedouins in the Middle East. Of these three breeds, only the Saluki comes in two coat varieties, smooth and feathered. The Azawakh and the Sloughi are always smooth-coated.

The more common feathered Saluki.

non-commercial racing and lure-coursing in France, Holland, Germany, Switzerland, Italy and Denmark, and more recently in

Chechia and Caiman du Simoun in the Jardin d'Acclimatation, France, in a picture from the 1920s.

Amulet von dek Burg Windeck, a German-bred bitch from the 1930s.

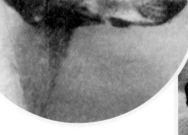

The correct Sloughi head, according to the French standard, 1938.

Algerian Sloughis, circa 1940s.

the US. As will become apparent, the breeding of Sloughis in Europe and the US is quite international, blending lines across borders. This breeding also includes, sometimes, African bloodlines representing all four countries of origin.

As we will see, the distinctiveness of the Sloughi as a separate breed was never a point of discussion in Europe as, in many countries, the breed was imported before the Saluki was. For example, in the Netherlands, the first Saluki arrived in 1924, some 20 years after the first Sloughi, and the first Afghan Hounds in 1936. It is only in the US and England, where the Saluki could be seen in its two different coats, smooth and feathered, that people argued, sometimes vehemently, that the Sloughi was nothing more than a smooth Saluki. All this in spite of the fact that one of the pioneers of the Saluki breed herself, the Honorable Mrs. Florence Amherst, who had seen these dogs in their countries of origin, clearly distinguished between the Sloughi and Saluki and was against interbreeding these two breeds. There are clear differences between these two breeds as well as the other sighthound breeds.

FRANCE
Unfortunately, some of the early history of the breed in France before 1970 has been lost as a result of a lack of record-keeping

The Sloughi Muska was imported into Holland in 1899 by Auguste Le Gras.

and the destruction of some of the archives of the Société Centrale Canine by a fire in the 1970s. However, an engraving in a book of dogs dated 1890 and several postcards and articles from the 1920s show us that the breed was treasured, particularly for coursing.

The breed's relationship with the French likely began with Algerian dogs and the French cavalry, who encountered the breed while stationed in Algeria. Toward the end of the 1880s, Général Daumas, who was fluent

Haoëesj was also imported into Holland by Mr. Le Gras in 1899.

in Arabic, became the consul of the Emir Abd-el-Kader, then was in charge of everything pertaining to the "indigenous Algerians." He wrote several books on the horses of the Sahara and the Arabian Society, which give us some of the best descriptions of the breed's role in Arabian society. Less inspired by the romanticism of the breed than was the artist Auguste Le Gras in Holland, the French officers were avid hunters who took advantage of the breed's great field abilities.

Another French horseman, Mr. Robert Mauvy, who later became president of the Sloughi Club in the 1970s, hunted gazelle and jackals with Sloughis in the desert between 1913 and 1928. It is from all of these reports that the first distinction was made between the more substantial mountain Sloughis and the finer-boned,

smaller desert Sloughis. In the 1940s, Charles Cornevin, Pierre Durel and then Xavier Przezdziecki wrote extensively about the breed in Algeria.

Through the Dutch records, we know of at least one French breeder before the 1930s, Mme. Simeon de Lavallart, who bred her last du Simoun Sloughi litter in 1928. Three of her dogs were imported into Holland: Caid du Simoun, born in 1928 (Kebir du Peroy out of Arad, co-breeder Delagrange); Zerga du Simoun, born in 1925 (Kebir du Peroy out of Taia) and Zanie du Simoun. Although she stopped breeding Sloughis, Mme. Simeon de Lavallart was still judging dogs in the 1970s.

Xavier Przezdziecki was stationed for several years in the Sahara desert in Algeria. In fact, he met his first Sloughi in Morocco in 1927. In 1929, fresh from the

A litter of Sloughis bred in 1911 in Holland.

cavalry school of Saumur, he took an assignment in the Sahara Desert, where he shared his life as a mehari (camel rider) with Sloughis. After a detour in 1933 to the Middle East (Iraq and Turkey), where he also hunted with the local sighthounds, he returned to the Sahara in 1937. He was given his first Sloughi, a bitch named Mitou, barely ten days old, as her mother had no milk. With much patience, Przezdziecki raised this bitch with camel milk. She was born in 1942 at the far end of Tanezrouf, from parents originating in southern Morocco. She was bred later with a dog from north-western Libya, her kids and grand-kids participating in the races of the racetracks in Algiers (*Cynodrome d'Alger*). His kennel prefix, de la Horde d'Or, was regis-tered by the Fédération Cynologique Internationale (FCI) in 1952. In 1954, Xavier Przezdziecki became president of the racing society (*Société d'encouragement aux courses de Sloughis et autres Lévriers*) and, with some friends, founded a group of racing Sloughis in Algiers.

During this time in France, the first breed standard was published by the French Sighthound Club in 1925. Later on the *Club du Sloughi* published an in-depth version in 1938. This club is now integrated in the *Club du Sloughi, des Levri-ers d'Afrique et du Galgo* (SLAG), the current club representing the

breed. The *Club du Sloughi* spon-sored this breed as a *Race française* or French breed. Morocco took over later in the 1970s (Standard # 188d, in Rabat), somewhat modifying the standard for the breed.

As in other European coun-tries, the breeding of Sloughis in France was interrupted during World War II, but resumed in the 1950s before the war between France and Algeria. Still, there were very few Sloughi breeders in France at the time. Two breeders who worked together in the 1950s and 1960s had occasional litters. They were Mrs. F. Stacul with the Sloughis d'Ymauville and Mrs. Sigaux with the Sloughis des Barines. Of particular interest to us are the Sloughis d'Ymauville. Many of the red brindle Sloughis today, whether in France or the US, descend, through the Kahloul de la Treille Sloughis, from one stud, Icare d'Ymauville (red brindle) and his two daughters Iowa (red brindle) and Isa Dora (red black brindle).

The Sloughis d'Ymauville included in their pedigrees four imports from Tunisia, Morocco and Algeria. The dog Y'Schrab (light sand-colored) had cropped-up ears and traditional brand marks on his front legs, and was imported from a Tunisian nomadic tribe. The bitch B'Douchka, sand with black mask and topaz eyes, was imported from the breeding of the

Glaoui of Marrakesh, Morocco. The dog T'Abdul Ahmid was imported from Tebessa, Algeria, and the red brindle Fautchy was assumed to come from there also. The Sloughis d'Ymauville were also related to Sloughis des Barines by the Sloughia ("sloughia" refers to bitches) Chechia Bent Abdul des Barines (red brindle with black mask, sired by T'Abdul Ahmid) and the Sloughis de la Horde d'Or, bred by Xavier Przezdziecki, then stationed in Algeria, through the Sloughias Alenda de la Horde d'Or (dam of Chechia Bent Abdul des Barines) and V'Paouk de la Horde d'Or, and the Sloughi W'Tchinguiz Kahn II de la Horde d'Or.

The two brindle daughters of Icare d'Ymauville, Iowa and Isa Dora, were bred by E. Rhode Goudineau to the dogs Ihran (sand with black mask) and Bahram Schuru-esch-Schams (red sand black mask, from the second litter bred by I. and E. Schritt in Germany). The dam of Bahram was Dutch Ifrita al Schams (red with black mask) and the sire was the Int. Fr. Ch. Sahib de la Ruine (sand with black mask). Sahib de la Ruine also sired the Libyan Sloughia Damiela in Holland. The Sloughis Kahloul de la Treille included later the Moroccan Sloughi Abd des Grimoires de Kerfa (sand with black mantle). His sire (Vick d'Ouled Dlim) and his dam (Viana D'Ouled Dlim) came from the Royal Kennels in Rabat, and were also sand with black mantle. Thus was the sand with black mask/black mantle introduced in France.

Xavier Przezdziecki returned to France in 1962, and soon thereafter the first litter of the Montouchet de la Horde d'Or Sloughis, bred by Agnes Rey, was born in France in 1964. Many of the Sloughis in France today descend from the d'Ymauville, the Kahloul de la Treille, the de la Horde d'Or and the Montouchet de la Horde d'Or Sloughis, as well as from German Sloughis through the Schuru-esch-Schams breeding. Although the Sloughis in France descend originally from dogs imported from the same countries as the Dutch and German Sloughis, the French preference for finer-boned Sloughis has led to a somewhat different type of Sloughi, sometimes referred to as the French Sloughi.

The breed in France is active in coursing, racing and conformation events. The first French World Winner for the breed was the red dog Malik in 1979, and the first French European Winner was the sand bitch Ulla del Ain Naga in 1974. In 1980, Malik, Mandane, Ô Kaline, Naiade, Jenna and Nitouche du Montouchet de la Horde d'Or were the first six Sloughis recognized for racing. These dogs ran distances of up to 900 meters.

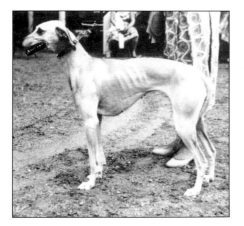

TOP LEFT: Gamera d'Ymauville, 1950s, sand black mask. TOP RIGHT: Chechia Bent Abdul des Barines, 1950s, red brindle. BOTTOM LEFT: Abd des Grimoires de Kerfa, black mantle. BOTTOM RIGHT: Massouah d'Ymauville, 1964.

HOLLAND

The best records about the very beginning of the breed in Europe are kept in the Netherlands. The story of the Sloughi (or "Sloeqi," as it was spelled at the time) starts in this country with the artist Auguste Le Gras. Fluent in Arabic, Le Gras traveled to North Africa and lived for a while in Chardaia, Algeria. In those days, the Sloughi was a purely romantic dog, fitting perfectly in the "Jugend style" era, with the sense of adventure and the love of foreign countries. The breed's origins in the African desert, images of the sheiks in their white floating djellabas, the Sloughi's ancient history and the dogs' elegant lines appealed to Le Gras's romantic imagination.

His foundation bitch, Muska ("the grabber"), was given to him as a present. She was born in Oeargla, Algeria, and was from a litter bred by the Marabout Sidi Mohammed Belkassem around 1896. Bred to a brindle dog, Sidi Sheig the First, Muska had a litter of nine pups in 1898 in Algeria

Two historic drawings of Sloughis. The top drawing is one of the first two European drawings of a Sloughi, done in 1890 by the well-known cynologist Pierre Mégnin in France. This Sloughi's parents came from Libya. The bottom drawing shows the Dutch artist Auguste Le Gras's rendition of the ideal Sloughi in 1900. This drawing was published in various articles in the early part of the 20th century.

before she was brought to Holland in November of that same year when Le Gras returned there. Her traveling companions were two of her own pups, her son Haoëesj ("strong one") and her daughter Oereïda ("little rose"). Le Gras showed these three Sloughis in Amsterdam in 1899 and, from that moment on, these dogs became legendary.

In 1900, Le Gras traveled once more to North Africa and brought back two more Sloughis to

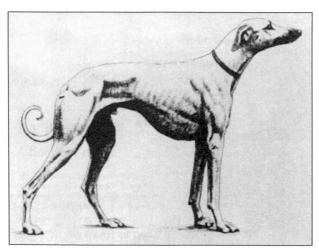

Holland. This time, they came from Tunisia. The dog Schaab ("nobleman") came from central Tunisia and the bitch Zeïna ("beautiful one") came from Tunis and was bred by Princess Fatima. Zeïna did not like Holland. A picture shows a shy, discontented animal and, within one year (July 1901), she had to be put down. She did, however, have one litter in Holland.

Dutch Sloughi breeding began in 1901 with three initial litters bred by Le Gras, blending Tunisian with Algerian lines: Zeina and Haoëesj (eight pups); Oereïda and Schaab (ten pups) and Muska and Schaab (nine pups). Haoëesj later went to the Sultan of Djakarta in Java. Oereïda was owned by Michel La Fontijn, the other influential figure in the Sloughi fancy in Holland (kennel Sahara). He bred three litters with her, each yielding about ten pups; the last two breedings were with Sidi Sheig II, her nephew.

Sidi Sheig II, out of the first litter, became a very famous dog, always mentioned as a champion; he was also owned by Michel La Fontijn. The pedigrees of almost all Sloughis of those pre-war days descend from the three initial litters bred by LeGras, as well as Sidi Sheig (I) and Muska. Ch. Sidi Sheig was mated to several bitches: Nagla, Zeïna II, Melika and Oase. On May 12,

1905, a litter was born by Ch. Sidi Sheig out of Zohra (a brother-sister combination). One of the bitches was named Oeargla, after Muska's birthplace. The breeder was J. Verver in Blaricum. Zohra died on June 19, 1916. On June 27, 1909, a litter was born at La Fontijn's kennel.

Within a few years, Sloughi breeding became a serious endeavor in Holland. Le Gras managed to raise enthusiasm for the breed in a great number of people. Within four years, this group of fanciers was large enough to found the Dutch Sloeqi Club in 1903, to start a stud book and to point out specific characteristics for the breed. The club's founders were Auguste Le Gras and Michel La Fontijn.

The Dutch Sloeqi Club issued at least three booklets about the breed; all three (in original or copy) are still kept in Holland. They contain the first breed standard, put together by Auguste Le Gras. The stud book devotes a full page to each dog registered, accompanied by many photos that prove invaluable to our understanding of Sloughi type at the time.

The Le Gras line was pure-bred for some 20 years. Breed recognition and championship status were achieved in 1906. By 1937, there were 340 Sloughis registered in Holland. The last pure-bred Le Gras descendant,

Ch. Tajoe van den Dar Es Sleg, died in 1929. None of this Dutch breeding survived World War II. The Sloughi's decline in Holland had begun prior to this, as some racing fanatics had crossed Sloughis with Greyhounds, and in the 1930s it had become difficult to find a pure-bred Sloughi. The Dutch Sloeqi Club imported three dogs from France to try to revive the breed. They were Caid du Simoun, Zerga du Simoun and Zanie (or Zamie) du Simoun. These Sloughis were bred by Mme. Simeon de Lavallart. Zanie was bred to Tajoe van den Dar Es Sleq at the van de Lindenhof kennel. Three pups were born on February 26, 1928, one of which, interestingly, was sand with a dark overlay.

The first Dutch Sloughi champion, Sidi Sheig II, pictured in early 1900.

The Dutch Sloeqi Club ceased activity toward the end of the 1930s. In the late 1920s, there was also a Sighthound Club Confederation for a short while. In 1935, this confederation split; fairly soon after that, there was no sign of life from the Sloeqi Club. Another club was founded in 1935, the Dutch Club for Oriental Sighthounds (NVOW), for all "Oriental" breeds. This club still exists today, and it adopted the Sloughi during the renaissance of the breed in Holland in the 1960s.

After World War II, the first litter in Holland was bred by Mr. Immig and was born on May 6, 1969 by Amen Ouled Nails from Switzerland out of the rescue Luuk. Out of this litter, the red bitch Ifrita al Schams was imported by Mr. and Mrs.

A Moroccan stamp featuring the Sloughi.

المملكة المغربية

البريد

2,00
POSTES

SLOUGHI   السلوقي

ROYAUME DU MAROC

LISETTE DELOOZ   1984

Schritt of the Schuru-esch-Schams kennel in Germany and became the dam of the second and third Schuru-esch-Schams litters, bred first with French Sahib de la Ruine, then with Quitus.

The bitch Damiela (also spelt Djameela) was imported by Heather van Duyvenbode from Libya in

1973. A sister of Tagiurie el Sian, first Sloughi imported to the US, bred by the Sian tribe, she had a litter of 13 puppies when bred to the French Sahib de la Ruine. Out of this litter, the bitch Amira el Cid is found in many Dutch pedigrees today.

The first Sloughi Dutch champion was Ch. Sidi Sheig. The first Dutch Junior World Winners were El Basshar and Al Hansa Van Klein Vossenburg. In 1980, the first Dutch FCI World Winners were Akbar of Mumtaz-I-Javanadmi, bred by Jeanny Brackmann, and Bluedon's Zaherit Eltofah; they were followed the next year by Al Sharif of Mumtaz-I-Javanadmi and PWCA

Mohamed Nagla. The Sloughi had become active in racing (lure-coursing did not exist in those days) around 1926; however, it was in 1989 that NVOW designed a dual champion title that combined conformation and performance results. The first dog and bitch to win this title were Beldi, three-time winner, and Barud Kamar al Akbar, five-time winner, owned by Els Siebel.

Today, if not very common, the breed is active in Holland mostly in conformation events, but a few dedicated owners take their dogs to coursing and racing events also. From the Le Gras dogs to today's Dutch Sloughis, the type of the

Algerian stamps, postmarked on the first day of issue, and envelope featuring the Sloughi.

breed in the Netherlands does not seem to have changed much. In 2002, the two Dutch stud books featured 340 Sloughis before 1940 and some 475 after 1966.

GERMANY

At the turn of the 20th century, some 31 Sloughis were registered in Germany. Mrs. E. Windecker-Castan of the von der Burg Windeck Kennel bred at least four litters in 1939 (Kabyle x Zohra), 1942 and 1943 (Kabyle x Ballade von der Burg Windeck), 1944 (Banner von der Burg Windeck x Ballade von der Burg Windeck). In fact, it seems that Prince August Wilhelm of Prussia himself must have had at least one Sloughi. A wonderful postcard from the late 1920s shows his son, Prince Alexander Ferdinand of Prussia, with his Sloughi-like dog (red with black mask). The brand marks on the dog's front legs suggest that he might have been imported from Algeria or Tunisia. However, as elsewhere, World War II brought an end to all breeding and other dog-related activities.

A renewal of interest in the breed was sparked in the early 1970s, and the first litter was born at the Schuru-esch-Schams kennel on December 23, 1971 out of Muna by the Swiss dog Berak Ouled Nails. The Schuru-esch-Schams "A" litter produced sand with black mask and brindle puppies. Another bitch, Ifrita al Schams (red with black mask), was imported from Holland and

subsequently bred to two Sloughis in France, Sahib de la Ruine and Quitus (imported from Algeria), giving the Schuru-esch-Schams kennel their second and third litters. Between 1971 and 1989, 87 Sloughi litters were born with a total of 594 puppies, which, together with the imports, resulted in 635 Sloughis' being registered in the German stud book.

Early country-of-origin imports to Germany were Vassya d'Ouled Dlim, Vero del Ksiri, Xoute des Oudaia, Cyril and Zouakha (Morocco), and Talit, Bedui and Amon Rha (Tunisia), later to be followed by U'Oued and U'Hlouwa des Hammadates de Merzougha and Mansur (Morocco). Early European imports were bitches Usti del Ain Naga, Urgande del Ain Naga and Tarbia (France), and Allascha Habib el Tunis, Sabra el Djerid (Switzerland). Dogs included El Basshar van Klein Vossenburg, Arbi van de Kirkelsberg and Furuq of Mumtaz-I-Javanadmi (Holland), Lewis and Leska (France) and Shaarawi el Djerid (Switzerland). Since then, many more litters have been born, blending various bloodlines from the various European countries, as well as country-of-origin dogs.

Modern reproductive techniques also played a role in German breeding. In May 2001, a litter of nine puppies was born as the result of the first successful artificial insemination in the breed in Germany. The litter was born at the Sheik el Arab

THE SLOUGHI AND THE GREYHOUND

Compared to the Greyhound, the Sloughi is built more on a square than on a rectangle (from withers to hips to hind feet to front feet), the Shoughi's forehead is larger and his ears are longer and drop on each side of the head. The ears of the Sloughi should not be folded and pushed back in a small "rose ear" as in the Greyhound. The coat colors of the Greyhound are more variable than in the Sloughi; the Greyhound's colors include large quantities of white, as well as dilute colors such as "blue," not accepted today in the Sloughi. In well-conditioned individuals of each breed, the Greyhound looks much more muscular and the Sloughi much leaner. The two breeds are of equal height, though the Greyhound is much heavier than the Sloughi. The Sloughi has a smooth, floating and effortless gait, tail held low, head at a moderate angle to the body. As a result of the squarish build and moderate angulation, there is no exaggeration in extension. The front paw does not reach beyond the tip of the nose. The Sloughi's racing style resembles that of the Greyhound, but because of its straighter topline, the Sloughi cannot flex its back as much as the Greyhound. On short distances, the Sloughi is slower than the Greyhound, with speed averaging 28–31 miles per hour; on long distances, the Sloughi overcomes the Greyhound, as it has greater stamina.

Sloughi.

Greyhound.

kennel (P. Lauer) out of Aljanah Sheik el Arab in Germany by Tunisian import Tarfa in the US. In June 2002, the first German litter sired by a Libyan dog, Dukal Umm Bersheba's el Abid, imported by the Swiss kennel Bersheba (Dieter Grams), was born at the Mahanajim kennel (Dr. S. Schlenkrich) out of Asira Mahanajim.

The first attendance of Sloughis at the World Dog Show took place in Germany (Dortmund, 1973) and saw littermates Aschkurak (sand brindle) and Afri Schuru-esch-Schams (sand with black mask) winning the adult titles, and Dutch imports to Germany El Basshar and Al Hansa van klein Vossenburg taking the Junior World Winner titles.

The Sloughi was recognized for racing in 1973. The first race took place in Hessen, with an entry of five Sloughis, and was won by

Arabeya Schuru-esch-Schams. In 1974, the Sloughi became an official breed in international racing. Coursing is a relatively new activity in Germany; the French-bred Jom el Ahir, owned by Iris Rolli, became the first coursing champion. The Sloughi in Germany long has been active in both conformation and performance venues. Some of the first Sloughis to combine top wins in conformation and performance were dogs Scha'iq Schuru-esch-Schams and Latif Schuru-esch-Schams, and bitch Chauda Schuru-esch-Schams.

SWITZERLAND

In 1896 Chouia, owned by Mr. Orcellet, became the first Sloughi to be registered in Switzerland. She was followed by Zina, owned by Captain Balay, in 1923. These two bitches were succeeded by the first male registered, Samson of Grevil, bred in England by Major Beswick and registered in 1931 by his owner M. Hurtig. Mr. Jutz (Ouled-Nails kennel) imported four Sloughis from Morocco to Switzerland in 1961; these were the dog Shidi Mechra-Bel-Ksiri (sand with black mask), his sister Suleika Mechra-Bel-Ksiri (sand with black mask), the dog Ain Rich and the bitch Fatima de Settat. Fatima de Settat whelped the first litter in Switzerland at Ouled-Nails in July 1966. The seven puppies were sired by Ain Rich, which included the dog Amen Ouled-Nails, who became a sire in Holland. The second litter, consisting of three puppies, followed in 1968. This litter produced the dog Berak Ouled-Nails (who sired Muna for the first litter of the German kennel Schuru-esch-Schams in 1971). The breeding at Ouled-Nails ceased after this second litter.

In 1976, two Sloughis were imported from Tunisia, the bitches Zina and Mascha. In 1977 the bitch Richa el Djerid was imported also from Tunisia by the El Djerid kennel. The third Swiss litter, of eight pups, was born at the Habib el Tunis kennel in March 1977, out of Mascha by Chalifa Schuru-esch-Schams. This litter included the well-known bitch Allasha Habib el Tunis. In January 1978, el Djerid kennel (Rosy Bächtiger) produced five puppies sired by Sharaf d'Ain Gh'Zel (imported from Germany) out of Richa el Djerid. In 1979, another Sloughi was imported from Tunisia, the dog Masoud. In April 1990, the Bersheba kennel (Dieter Grams) produced its first litter, out of Béguine du Montouchet de la Horde d'Or by Ibn Jamil Mumtaz-I-Javanadmi.

The Swiss Sloughi breeding blends bloodlines of very varied origins. Several dogs were imported from other European countries as well as from the countries of origin, with kennel names such as Montouchet de la Horde d'Or, Kahloul de la Treille, de Slouaz and Magistère in France; Schuru-esch-Schams, D'Ain Gh'Zel, el Athal, Nuri al Baida, el Maschrak and Min

Ahrar al Maghrib in Germany; Mumtaz-I-Javanadmi in Holland and Intissar in Italy. More recent imports from the countries of origin include Yado ben Sayed from Morocco and Dukal umm Bersheba el Abid from Libya.

In Switzerland the Sloughi breed is mostly active in conformation events. The first Swiss champion dog and bitch were D'Jasir el Djerid and D'Jadine el Djerid; the first FCI International Champion was D'Jasir el Djerid; the first World Winner was D'Jadine el Djerid (1984); the first Junior World Winner was Shaarawi el Djerid (1985); the first European Winner was Sabra el Djerid (1989); the first Junior European Winner was Ardan Habib el Tunis (1978); the first country-of-origin dog to finish a championship title was Dukal umm Bersheba el Abid (2001).

Probably the first Sloughi to have completed a racing license was Uddah in 1972 (owned and bred by the author) on the racing track of Versoix. Uddah also participated at the international race in Geneva (Versoix) in 1973, being the first Sloughi to do so in Switzerland. Sloughis participated later again at a national race, the Züri-Meisterschaft, Rifferswil, on May 18, 1980. The breed is represented by the Swiss Club for the Sloughi and the Azawakh [*Schweizerischer Club für Sloughi und Azawakh* (SCSA)], and its stud book has around 200 Sloughis registered.

Saluki.

THE SLOUGHI AND THE SALUKI

Although they were considered to be different breeds in Europe and in England during the first third of the 20th century, this situation changed during the second half of the 20th century, when the Sloughi became often mistaken with the smooth variety of the Saluki. The Sloughi and the Saluki (smooth or feathered) are different breeds, genetically different and of different origins. In fact, anybody with a basic background in anatomy who takes the time to objectively compare the two breeds will be struck by the important differences, best listed as follows:

The Saluki is bred in a large variety of coat colors, including colorations with various quantities of white. The Sloughi, in contrast, is allowed to exist only in the various shades of sand to fawn with or without black markings such as a black mask (often with dark ears), brindle, black mantle or dark overlay. In fact, the two most common coat colors of the Sloughi, brindle and sand with black mask, are either uncommon in or not cited for the Saluki.

The Saluki is represented by two different varieties according to hair length, the feathered and the smooth. It is possible that both coat types can be found in the same litter. In contrast, the Sloughi is always smooth. It is interesting to note here that smooth sighthounds imported from the Middle East sometimes produce offspring with long silky hair. This is one reason that smooth sighthounds imported from that region are not registered directly as Sloughis in Germany, whereas those from Morocco, Algeria, Tunisia and Libya are. The long silky hair (feathering) is inherited recessively in the Saluki breed; feathered Salukis very rarely produce smooth puppies, but smooth Salukis can produce feathered pups. Because it is very difficult to get rid of a recessive gene and because Sloughis from North Africa never produce feathered offspring indicate that the Sloughi and the Saluki are genetically different not only in the inheritance of coat colors but also in the length of coat.

Sloughi.

The Sloughi, particularly the mountain type, is a bigger, more substantial dog than the Saluki. Sloughis, particularly males, have larger and stronger heads, are usually bigger and look more powerful than Salukis and Azawakhs. The Saluki has a light and effortless gait, in which the degree of reach and drive varies between the extreme extension, with the front paws reaching beyond the tip of the nose, of some modern show dogs, and the more moderate gait of the so-called "old fashioned" and "desert-breds," which resemble more closely that of the Sloughi. As in the Sloughi, the Saluki's tail is held low and the head is at a normal angle to the body.

The studies by Bruchmüller of the blood of various sighthounds (Afghan, Borzoi, Saluki, Sloughi, Azawakh) found, according to the allele distribution, a specific genetic profile for each breed. In contrast to all other breeds investigated, the Sloughi and the Azawakh, both of African origin, have an additional allele on the GPI (glucose phosphate isomerase) locus.

The geographical distribution of the two breeds is also different. The Sloughi is found in North Africa (Morocco, Algeria, Tunisia, Libya), and the Saluki in the Middle East (Saudi Arabia, Israel, Iran, Iraq and Turkey). The Sloughi is the sighthound of the Berber people, the Saluki the sighthound of the Bedouin.

Finally, confusion has not been improved by semantics. Basically the words "Slughi" (colloquial Arabic) and "Saluki" (classical Arabic) mean the same thing, nothing more than "windhound" or "sighthound." These two different breeds were named Sloughi and Saluki, respectively, by the Fédération Cynologique Internationale. In the countries of origin, the local people add an adjective to "Slughi/Saluki" and refer to these breeds as as Slughi-shami/Slughi-nedji (feathered and smooth Saluki), Slughi-mogrebi (Sloughi) and Slughi-inglisi (Greyhound), for example. They do the same as we do when we add an adjective to our word "sighthound," and refer to these breeds as Persian Sighthound (Saluki), Arabian Sighthound (Sloughi) and English Sighthound (Greyhound).

FINLAND

The first Sloughi in Finland was the bitch Bou-Manjineni [by Shab Ben Eldjazaer (Algeria) out of Richa Talata (Algeria)], imported by Aili Porvali of Golden-West kennel from Gudrun Boulechfar in Sweden. Bou-Manjineni had two litters by sires imported from Sweden in 1971, the first by Fin. & Swed. Ch. Serdouk in 1972 and the second by Quargla-Etnen (Serdouk's son) in 1973. The first litter produced Ahmed, who became the first Finnish-bred International Champion. By 1978, there were 9 litters and 61 registrations. Seven litters were bred by Aili Porvali, one by Hellin Hyökki and one by Ansa Tapaninen. These litters were all closely related, as they resulted from breeding between the two Golden-West litters.

Somehow the interest in Sloughis died after the 1970s, and it was almost two decades before Pia and Hannu Puomila imported a bitch, Tiri Schuru-esch-Schams, from Germany in 1991, and Usdan Schuru-esch-Schams in 1992. Jaana Hyväri imported a bitch, El Sissa Min Darazzja Loewwla, from Holland at the end of 1992.

Aili Porvali and Pia Puomila co-bred a litter between Tiri and Usdan in 1995, the Golden-West "H" litter of ten puppies, all of which astonishingly became champions. Usdan also sired the first Tillieville (Ingela Näslund) litter in Sweden with Norwegian Arhib's Asiir Bintu Hadjib. From this litter, a bitch, Tillieville Zim Salabim, was imported to Finland.

In 1999, for the first time in the history of the breed, intercontinental artificial insemination with frozen semen was carried out with multi-Ch. of Golden-West Hannah by Ch. Ghali Shi'Rayân from the US. Nine puppies were born on May 15, 1999 at the Syringa kennel (Eva Hildorsson) in Sweden. Two puppies of this litter, Syringa Heritage (Paivi Nurmi) and Syringa Harmony (Anna-Mari Rönkkö/Pia Puomila), were imported to Finland. Syringa Happiness was imported to the US by Shi'Rayân and became the first European-bred Sloughi to win an American racing title in 2000. Syringa Heritage was the top Sloughi in Finland in 2000 and 2001. Syringa Harmony set a milestone in coursing by receiving the first coursing certificate in Finland and becoming the first Sloughi to win the Derby in 2002.

Other imports came from the US, Germany and Morocco, including Hulkah Shi'Rayân (1998), owned by Pia and Hannu Puomila, and Jaraa Shi'Rayân (2000), owned by Tarja Matikainen. Hulkah Shi'Rayân became the first American-bred Sloughi to become a Swedish, Finnish and International Champion in Europe. She is the foundation bitch of the La'Jahhibu kennel (Pia Puomila and Anna-Mari Rönkkö). There are approximately 100 Sloughis registered in Finland.

SWEDEN

At the end of the 1960s Gudrun Boulechfar imported several Sloughis from Algeria. The first male was cropped, bad-tempered and of doubtful ancestry, while the bitch Richa Talata represented a very appealing type. She won a few first prizes and later got a suitable partner in the French-imported male Serdouk, who in 1971 became the first Swedish champion of the breed. Between them, they produced the first Swedish-born Sloughi to become a champion, the dog Quargla-Etnen. When Boulechfar left Sweden, her dogs were exported to other breeders, first to Finland and then to England where they became foundation dogs for the breed. The entire breed population in Sweden after that consisted of a few dogs bred by the Boulechfars and sold to other fanciers. Some 20 years later, interest in the breed was revitalized. In 1996 the first litter was born at the Tillieville kennel of Ingela Näslund (out of Norwegian import Arhib's Asiir Bintu Hadjib by German import to Finland Usdan Schuru-esch-Schams). Nine pups were born to Ch. of Golden-West Hannah by Ch. Ghali Shi'Rayân from the US. This is the aforementioned historic litter, bred by artificial insemination with frozen semen, born on May 15, 1999 at the Syringa kennel of Eva Hildors-

In 1973, Tagiurie el Sian, from Libya, became the first Sloughi imported into the US. Shown with owner Kate Rodarty.

Tagiurie el Sian's litter sister Damiela, a foundation bitch in Holland circa 1973.

son. Today Sweden's Sloughi breeding is based on imports from Germany, France and Italy. Swedish Sloughis participate in shows, coursing, agility and tracking.

THE SLOUGHI IN THE UNITED STATES AND CANADA

Probably the first Sloughi in the US was Tagiurie El Sian, a dog brought into the country from Libya in 1973 by Kate and Carl Rodarty. The Rodartys of California acquired Tagiurie, and their Dutch friends, the van Duyvenbodes acquired his sister, Djameela (Damiela in the Dutch stud book). Tagiurie was sand with a faint mask, a typical Libyan desert Sloughi. While cherished by his owners, he was not bred, because of his age and the absence of a possible mate. He died in 1979. Djameela had one litter in 1971 and a record litter of 13 puppies in 1973 when she was bred to the Fr. & Int. Ch. Sahib de la Ruine.

In 1979, Carole Cioce, also of California, imported two German Sloughis, Picaro Schuru-esch-Schams (sand-colored male) and Nisa Schuru-esch-Schams (red with black mask). In 1982, Picaro was entered in Mexican shows and won the first Mexican championship title for the breed. Carole Cioce had also done some preliminary work in order to start an American Sloughi Club, but this idea was not brought to fruition until later.

In 1981, the first litter of Sloughis, of littermates Phitoussi and Pharaonne Kahloul de la Treille, was born at the de Moreau kennel, then in California. In 1988, the first litter out of which

dogs were to be shown was born at Mario Rechzaid's home. The parents were Fahran of Mumtaz-I-Javanadmi and Tounsia Kahloul de la Treille. One bitch of this litter, Jaaram Nubia, introduced the breed to the sighthound fancy.

In 1987, a rare-breed exhibit sponsored by the Rare Breed Kennel Club (RBKC) was organized in collaboration with the Kennel Club of Beverly Hills. Jack McGuffin represented the Sloughi with his bitch Jaaram Nubia and had a booth with information about the breed. Along with the contacts established before, during and after this show, the Sloughi Fanciers Association of America (SFAA) was officially founded on January 1, 1988, and the stud book was opened. The founders were Gisela Cook-Schmidt, Jack McGuffin, Carole Cioce and Mario Rechzaid. Mrs. Moreau-Sipiere created the American Sloughi Association (ASLA) in 1989, after leaving the SFAA.

In April 1993, the first litter was born at the Shi'Rayân kennel, out of Fehda Fayrouz Kahloul de la Treille by German import Damir el Tahiri. Three of the four puppies of the Shi'Rayân "A" litter, Amir, Aswad and A'ssissa, established milestones for the breed in America.

Today, the SFAA is the premier and oldest American Sloughi club. Its specific aim is to preserve form and function, and thus genetic soundness, in the Sloughi. Its members have actively shown the Sloughi at dog shows and won top awards. The SFAA succeeded in getting the breed recognized by the National Oval Track Racing Association (NOTRA, non-commercial oval racing) in 1994 and by the American Sighthound Field Association (ASFA, lure coursing) in 2001. As a result, the Sloughi became a foundation breed of the Large Gazehound Racing Association (LGRA), created by Jack William Lewis of Rheata Whippets in 1995 to satisfy the requests of Sloughi owners to enable their breed to compete in sprint racing. The very first LGRA meet took place in 1995 in Utah at the Rheata Whippets Racing Group. It was launched by eight Sloughis and won by Amir Shi'Rayân. The Sloughi is also an official breed of the National Open Field Coursing Association (NOFCA) with the help of Vicki Clarke, and of the North American Coursing Association (NACA) for open field hunts. The Nubia Memorial Cup, donated to the SFAA by Jack McGuffin in 1995, is awarded each year to the number-one performing Sloughi in all venues combined.

All Sloughis of the SFAA are registered with the AKC Foundation Stock Service, which has been open to all rare breeds since 1995. The SFAA organized the first Sloughi specialty show,

> **CALIFORNIA, HERE I COME!**
> Probably the very first representation of a North African sighthound is found in *Harper's* magazine, published in 1882. This engraving pictures two mountain-type Sloughis on a leash. However, it was many more years before live Sloughis entered North America. As will become apparent, their story on this continent was quite international from the very beginning. California is the state in which most of the major early events concerning this breed took place.

together with the States Kennel Club, in Texas in 1997; the first Sloughi specialty in Canada, together with the Ontario Rare Breed Club, in Woodstock, Ontario in 1998; and the first Sloughi specialty in Lompoc, California, a showcase event of the Western Combined Sighthound Specialties in 1999. This was the largest specialty in the history of the breed and was judged by Mr. Bo Bengtson. In 2001, for the first time, a sprint-racing event was organized in conjuction with the SFAA national specialty. It was sponsored by the St. Louis Area Sighthound Club (SLASH), under the auspices of the Large Gaze-hound Racing Association, and took place on the Purina Farms track in Gray Summit, Missouri. In 2004, the American Kennel Club welcomed 17 other FSS rare breeds in its agility, obedience and tracking events. The AKC enables the Sloughi to participate in its coursing events as well.

Since the 1980s, other Sloughis have been imported from France (Kahloul de la Treille, de la Cité du Guerrier and de la Horde d'Or), Holland (Mumtaz-I-Javanadmi), Germany (Schuru-esch-Schams, el Tahiri, Sheik el Arab Mahanajim and Nuri al Baida), Italy (Intissar), Sweden (Syringa), Tunisia (Rym Cassandra and Tarfa) and Algeria (Richa and Ramla). Through these dogs, other lines were represented such as the French Ben Bahram, the Dutch Min Darazja Loewwla and El Cid, the Swiss el Djerid and the Moroccan Ouled Laouichat. Thus, most European and country-of-origin bloodlines are represented in the American Sloughi today.

Milestones in the show ring are listed as follows: the first FCI champion was Picaro Schuru-esch-Schams, owned by Carole Cioce; the first exhibit in the US was Jaaram Nubia in 1987, owned by Jack McGuffin; the first champion and first Group winner in the US was A'ssissa Shi'Rayân in 1994, owned by the author; the first Best in Show was Aswad Shi'Rayân in 1994, owned by the author; the first Best in Show bitch was Faraasha Shi'Rayân in 1998, owned by Jennifer Newman; the first Best in Specialty Show in the US was Aswad Shi'Rayân in 1997; the first Best in Specialty Show in Canada was Ghali Shi'Rayân in 1998, owned by the author; the first Best Puppy in Show was El Emin Schuru esch Schams, in Canada in 1996, owned by the author; the first Best in Specialty Show bitch was Shi'Rayân's Iswaar at Mazoe in 2001, owned by Ann Chamberlain and the author; and the first American-bred FCI International Champions were Aswad Shi'Rayân and A'ssissa Shi'Rayân.

Milestones in racing are listed as follows: the first Oval Racing Champion, first Supreme Oval Racing Champion and for many years highest pointed Sloughi in the NOTRA was Amir Shi'Rayân; the first Supreme Oval Racing

When a group of Sloughis is together, the dogs retain many pack behaviors, playing and staying nearby in the same general area.

Champion bitch was Bouthayna Shi'Rayân; the first Gazehound Racing Champion and first Superior Gazehound Racing Champion bitch was A'ssissa Shi'Rayân; the first Superior Gazehound Racing Champion was Aswad Shi'Rayân; the first Sloughi Superior Gazehound Racing Champion II, III & IV, first Sloughi number-one all-breeds in sprint racing and highest pointed sighthound in the LGRA was Fahel Shi'Rayân in 2001; the first European import racing champion was Syringa Happiness at Shi'Rayân; and the first country-of-origin Sloughi racing champion was Rym Cassandra.

The author, Dôminique de Caprona of Shi'Rayân Sloughis, is proud to have many milestones in lure coursing, including the first coursing champion, A'ssissa Shi'Rayân; the highest pointed Sloughi in the ASFA, Bouthayna Shi'Rayân; the first European import coursing champion, Chamisa Schuru-esch-Schams; and the first country-of-origin coursing champion, Rym Cassandra.

There are three stud books in the US in which Sloughis are registered: the SFAA stud book (since 1988), the ASLA stud book (since 1989) and the AKC Foundation Stock Service registry (since 1995). The AKC stud book is the largest, as it combines the clubs' stud books to some extent, with 275 dogs registered as of July

The spectacular sight of a Sloughi in flight. Aside from being a joy to watch, it's no wonder the breed is a record-setter in racing and coursing events.

2002. In addition, the Sloughi breed is also permitted to be shown under the auspices of the States Kennel Club, the United Kennel Club, the International All Breeds Canine Association and the American Rare Breed Association (ARBA).

By the end of 2000, shortly after a German scientific team discovered the gene responsible for progressive retinal atrophy (PRA) in the Sloughi, the Sloughi Fanciers Association of America worked together with OptiGen in the US to develop the same test in the Western Hemisphere. As of 2001, all dogs registered with the SFAA have to show proof of genotyping for PRA, and only the litters resulting from two PRA-clear animals, or from a PRA carrier with a PRA-clear animal, are registered with the SFAA. The Sloughi Fanciers Association of American and the United Kennel Club have accepted an American standard for the Sloughi, effective as of 2002.

THE SLOUGHI IN GREAT BRITAIN
According to Lady Florence Amherst, the first Sloughis were imported to England at the beginning of the 20th century by Mr. H. C. Brooke and were bred by Captain J. P. T. Allen. In fact, a stuffed Sloughi from that era was presented with an Afghan Hound and a Saluki by the Natural History Museum in Tring, Hertfordshire. Lady Amherst clearly considered these various populations of Slughi-shami, Slughi-yamani, Slughi-omani, Slughi-nedji and Slughi of the Sahara (Slughi-mogrebi) to be distinct, relying on the Arabs themselves, who considered these various groups of dogs to be different from one another. Lady Amherst's findings read as follows:

"Though different types are found in the same localities, natives are very careful not to mix the breeds...It should be the object of all those who import the Greyhounds of the East and breed them in this country, to try to keep distinct the different varieties, which in many cases have been so carefully preserved in their own lands. The historic interest attached to each breed is alone a sufficient inducement to do so."

Unfortunately, her wise advice was ignored, and it did not take long for the opinion to develop in England after World War II that all of these distinct breeds were one and the same breed, namely the Saluki. Adding to the confusion, important French books such as *Les Chevaux du Sahara et les Moeurs du Desert* by Général Daumas, which described the Algerian Sloughis' importance in the Algerian society at the end of the 19th century, were translated into English by simply replacing the word "Sloughi" in the original text with "Saluki." In 1969, Mr. and Mrs Waters wrote: "Today the Salukis of North Africa, Arabia, Syria, Persia and the steppes are all recognized as being of the same breed and of only two varieties, smooth coated and feathered...(The) officers of the French army returning from Algiers, where the French had been established for half a century, occasionally brought back with them Salukis bred in the Sahara desert." These statements are in total contradiction of the fact that these dogs had always been smooth and had always been referred to as Sloughis.

So it seems that whereas most of Europe agreed with Lady Amherst that the Sloughi of North Africa was a breed different from the Persian and Afghan sighthound breeds, some of her own countrymen denied the importance of her keen observations.

Mrs. Hope Waters seems to have changed her mind about the Sloughi and Saluki's being the same breed. Later, Sir Terence Clark, together with Gail Goodman in the US, continued arguing in that same vein during the last third of the 20th century. They completely confused the Sloughi breed, a more substantial and always smooth North African sighthound, with the Middle Eastern Salukis, which are found in both smooth and feathered varieties. Still today, the Sloughi breed is granted only "rare breed" status in the UK and US, and some crossbreeding between the Sloughi and the smooth Saluki still occurs, further blurring the distinction between the two breeds. After World War II, the first Sloughis were imported from Sweden in 1972 and became the foundation of the Djaeser kennel of R. Morland Austin. They were International Ch. Serdouk, sand black mask, born in 1969 in France, bred by Lieutenant Colonel J. Gaston (by Khalife out of Rani) and the bitch Richa Talata, brindle, born in 1964 in Algeria, by Saiyed out of Richa Etnen, bred by Mimoun Seliem Batna. While these two Sloughis were in quarantine, four puppies were born, the first Djaeser litter. It seems that Richa Talata had been bred to Shab Ben El Djaeser in Sweden prior to traveling.

Other imports to the UK included Al Machumba and Al Mufalma Mumtaz-I-Javanadmi in 1980 by J. Saunders and L. Paterson (Kamet); Murad Schuru-esch-Schams in 1997 and Taslima Schuru-esch-Schams in 1999 by P. Marston-Pollock (Falconcrag); Ullan de Moreau in 2000 by M.Goodman (Akh-Anubis); Intissar Ghazi and Rais Siyada Sani Shams in 2001 by P. Marston-Pollock (Falconcrag); and Rais Siyada Samra Soumrade in 2001 by S. Bamford (Doocloone).

Mr. Nicholas Morland Austin (Djaeser) enabled England's Kennel

DNA STUDY

The study of mitochondrial DNA of many dog breeds by Dr. Savolainen reveal that Sloughis and Salukis are genetically distinct and different in their genetic relationships to other breeds. Lady Florence Amherst's advice some 100 years ago to carefully preserve the special heritage of these two separate breeds proves to have been in the end the most knowledgeable. The Sloughi is not more related to the Saluki than it is to the Scottish Deerhound, Dachshund, Samoyed, Basenji or Boxer.

Club to accept the breed by providing proof of pure breeding of his Sloughis with registration papers from other recognized registries. The Sloughi Club was established in 1999, once it had the required 25 members, and the stud book has been open since 1972. The Kennel Club has its own standard for the breed. As of 2002, the Sloughi was still an Interim breed with The Kennel Club and therefore cannot yet compete for Championship Certificates (required to earn a championship in the UK).

The first Sloughi breed classes in the UK were held on April 13, 1974 at the Hunting Dogs of Ancient Egypt Open Show. Littermates Djaeser Patchouli Etnen (red brindle) and Djaeser Magda Wahad (brindle) were Best of Breed and Best of Opposite Sex. There are approximately 200 Sloughis registered with The Kennel Club.

THE SLOUGHI AND THE AZAWAKH

The Sloughi and the Azawakh are closely related. Whereas the Sloughi is the North African sighthound of the Berber people, the Azawakh is the Central African sighthound of the Touareg, as well as the Peul and Sonrai, people. The Touareg are themselves a Berber tribe that retreated from North Africa to Central Africa, probably taking with them their Sloughi-like dogs. In ancient times, they controlled the trans-Sahara caravan routes, taxing the goods they helped to convey and sometimes raiding neighboring tribes. In more recent times, these traditions were subdued by the French, who ruled Algeria.

The Sloughi is found in Morocco, Algeria, Tunisia and Libya, whereas the Azawakh is found between the countries of Mali and Niger, in the Azawakh Valley, Burkina Faso, Chad. There are some Azawakhs in Algeria. Over the years, through the extreme conditions south of the Sahara, and the geographical barrier of the desert, the two breeds have evolved into the two different breeds we know today.

Considering the structure of the breed, the Azawakh is built on a standing rectangle. The withers are apparent, the hips slightly higher than, or level with, the withers. The croup is bony and the brisket is deep but does not reach the elbow. The underline first falls and then rises sharply (keel). The ears are larger than the Sloughi's, but smaller than the Saluki's. The angulation is even more moderate than the Sloughi's. The expression of the breed's almond eyes is intense and somewhat feral. The coat is always smooth.

In Europe, the first Azawakhs were probably imported in the early 1970s from Mali. These Azawakhs, African sighthounds with their hanging ears and smooth coats, were first considered to be a variety of the Sloughi. Sloughis and Azawakhs were then presented together in shows and were both judged according to the Sloughi standard of that time. However, the Azawakh was never completely accepted as a Sloughi by the Sloughi breeders, particularly because of its white markings and different temperament. The various efforts to find a different name for this new "kind" of Sloughi show that, from the very beginning, people saw a difference between the two sighthounds. The Azawakh was first named "lévrier du Mali," then "oska," then "lévrier Touareg" (1974), then "lévrier de l'Azawakh" (1975) and then simply "Azawakh." As early as 1972, the *Windhundkommission* (Sighthound Commission) in Germany advised not to interbreed the two, awaiting a final decision concerning the status of the Azawakh. The differences in gait, proportion, coloration, temperament and geographical origin justified a separate standard for the Azawakh. It was established in France and accepted by the FCI in 1980.

The Azawakh has a flashy and springy gait, head and tail held high. As a result of the rectangular structure and very moderate angulation, there is no exaggeration in extension and the racing style is an upright gallop. Later, in Germany, Azawakhs were found to be slightly slower on the racetracks than the Sloughi and the Saluki.

In their countries of origin, the Sloughis, the Azawakhs and the Salukis fulfill similar functions and are highly treasured. They protect the herds from jackals, hunt on desert plains and guard their owners' property. The Azawakh is perhaps the fiercest guard of the three.

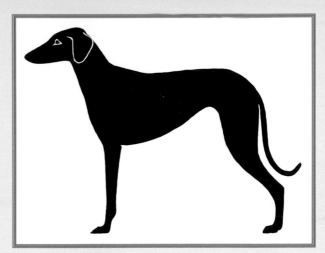

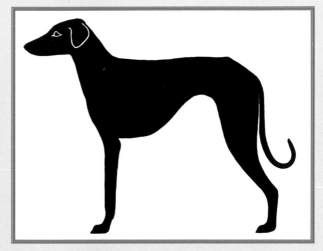

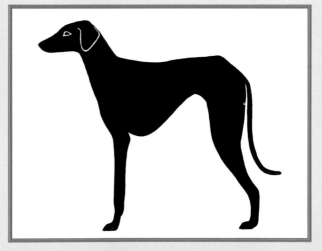

ABOVE: Azawakh.
TOP RIGHT: Outline of a Saluki.
MIDDLE RIGHT: Outline of a Sloughi.
BOTTOM RIGHT: Outline of an Azawakh.
The differences between these breeds
are often very subtle.

CHARACTERISTICS OF THE
SLOUGHI

The Sloughi is a tall, lean and noble-looking sighthound with a gentle, melancholy expression. He is built for chasing prey at full speed over long distances in open spaces. In Africa, Sloughis hunt all kinds of game, from grasshoppers, rodents, rabbits and desert hares to gazelles, jackals, boars and, in the old days, even hyenas. In general, they hunt "furry" game, but they catch birds as well. Outside Africa, they have adjusted to hunting other local game. They seem to dislike any kind of bird of prey, which they will relentlessly chase as the birds fly above them. When several Sloughis are confronted with snakes, they circle them. Some have been known to kill snakes, and, fortunately, all the stories known to the author involved non-poisonous snakes.

In North Africa, it is an all-around working breed, used for hunting as well as guarding the herds and the owner's property. The Sloughi is thus one of the few guarding sighthound breeds, with a keen sense of who is a stranger and who is not. He is not friendly like a Golden or Labrador Retriever. Because he

loves to run and has been bred to hunt in large open spaces for centuries, the Sloughi tends to roam. This is not a breed that you can leave unattended for long periods of time in the yard, nor can you allow it off leash in

"SLUGHI OF THE SAHARA"

In Great Britain, it is probably through the descriptions of various sighthounds by Lady Florence Amherst that the dog fancy became aware of the group of various dog populations referred to as *Slughi*—colloquial Arabic for "sighthound." Among the various breeds that she encountered during her travels, she referred to one of them as the "Slughi of the Sahara," the breed we know today as the Sloughi.

the neighborhood. The same applies to unfenced areas with game. Once hunting, it takes hours for a Sloughi to consider coming back to his owner. Sloughis have very keen vision, fine hearing and an excellent sense of smell. They are very good trackers that can flush game as well as chase it. Even as puppies, they are always on the alert for moving objects—even a leaf in the wind will trigger a chase. Sloughis playing together will

Sloughis resting afield, still staying in a loose pack.

often chase each other. They are the most wonderfully skilled running athletes and, although beautiful when lounging on a couch, they are breathtaking in action.

Sloughis have retained all of their instincts and, when several live together, they establish hierarchies stabilized by subtle behavioral rituals. Intentions and moods are expressed by a large repertoire of postures, expressions and sounds. Bitches have no problems whelping and nurturing their puppies well. Male dogs are often very protective of puppies. Sloughis are pack animals that love body contact and often sleep in piles. They love to do that with their owners also and delight in sharing a bed or couch.

Sloughis dig dens to cool off in hot weather, when they nurture puppies or just for fun. These dens can be as deep as 3 to 4 feet in the ground, with a chamber of some 4 to 5 feet under the earth. For this reason, the Sloughi is not always the ideal guest in a perfectly manicured yard, as the soft soil in flower beds is so much fun to dig into! Berbers and Bedouins sometimes dig comfortable spots in the sand for their Sloughis and cover them with blankets.

A Sloughi must be taken out to meet other people and animals beginning at an early age. He must be thoroughly socialized and integrated into all aspects of family life. Such a Sloughi becomes affectionate, gentle, playful and very loyal to his owner. Most bond very closely with one particular person and do not adapt easily to changes in ownership. Sloughis are cautious with strangers, whom they typically observe for a while before approaching. They usually do not like to be touched by strangers and often require some training to tolerate it.

Sloughis are excellent watchdogs, even when away from home. They protect what they perceive as their own, whether it's their owner's car or picnic blanket. A Sloughi may protect the area around his owner if, for example, the owner has been sitting outside for a while in the same spot with his Sloughi nearby on a leash. This ability must have been developed in the breed during centuries of nomadic life, as they needed to protect the owner's ever-changing home.

Sloughis raised in kennel situations, with little socializing, are typically very shy. They are nervous and scared, and they freeze in new situations; they may even snap, having never established a trusting relationship with people. They can be made to adjust to new situations, little by little and with a lot of time and patience. Well-socialized Sloughis

COAT OF MANY COLORS
The Sloughi exists in different coat colors. The most common are the sand with black mask and the sand brindle, but Sloughis can also be found in all shades, from mahogany red to pale sand, with or without brindling, black mask, black ears, black mantle and dark overlay. The brindle dogs can vary from very densely brindle (black brindle) to sparsely brindle. The darkest coat color is red brindle with black mantle and black mask.

can also get scared, but they rely on their trust in their owners to adjust to changing environments.

Sloughis are intelligent, curious and independent. They

The Sloughi is not always on the go; he is equally adept at providing quiet companionship and makes a great friend with whom to relax.

can be well trained if disciplined fairly, consistently and gently, as they are sensitive to anger. Dominant animals need a firm, yet never rough, hand. Although Sloughis do well in obedience, tracking, agility, racing, coursing and therapy work, they do not always take to training as easily as breeds like the Golden Retriever and Border Collie do. Sloughis typically need a lot of space around them and do not tolerate long hours of crating.

Sloughis love children who have been brought up to respect animals. They become quite protective of them. They get along well with other pets such as dogs, cats and parrots. Commonsense precautions are necessary, though, so remember that you must never leave a Sloughi, or any other dog, for long periods of time unattended with young children. Children can abuse dogs without realizing it, and a Sloughi (like any other dog) might want at some point to defend himself. Also

beware of children who might run away, screaming at the top of their lungs, as this will trigger a chase (as in any other sighthound). With small dogs that scurry and bark a lot, Sloughis tend to be edgy. Because they are tall, they may inadvertently be too strong when playing or running around with small dogs. Sloughis can become friends with cats, but may mistake their feline friends for game outside, particularly if the cat runs away. Some cats attack dogs and can inflict serious damage to the dog's eyes and face with their claws. Similar caution is required with Sloughis and parrots. A fluttering parrot may activate the hunting instinct of a Sloughi, and the beak of a large parrot can turn into a dangerous weapon.

Young Sloughis need lots of play outside where they can romp, dig and run as they please, along with plenty of toys and things to chew. Once he has had his daily run, an adult Sloughi will be perfectly happy to relax in the most comfortable spot in the house and watch the household from a distance. The older Sloughi needs a walk and gentle exercise to keep in shape. Regular exercise and being integrated into the family are prerequisites for a well-adjusted Sloughi.

Sloughis love to travel and be taken to different places with their owners. Conversely, it is a bad idea to leave a Sloughi to his

Sloughi owners never ceased to be amazed at their dogs' athletic feats.

Sloughis are not well suited to cold temperatures and should never be outdoors in the cold for too long. Some owners help their Sloughis stay warm in the winter with stylish doggie sweaters.

An interesting pet pack! The family pet parrot keeps watch over his Sloughi housemates, cuddled up together.

own devices in the yard. Bored Sloughis will look for their own entertainment, not necessarily close to the house. They can easily dig under fences to escape or jump over fences up to 6 feet high.

The Sloughi is a hound of the desert. He is unhappy in wet and cold surroundings. Although the dog develops a denser coat in winter, he should not be left outside for long periods of time in cold weather or in the rain. Sloughis enjoy a quick race in the snow, but need to come back in the house to warm up.

Sloughis often scream over minor injuries but become very stoic and silent when experiencing more serious pain, unless it becomes excruciating. For this reason, it is sometimes difficult to realize that the Sloughi is seriously ill or suffering, and to determine the cause in a timely manner. Like many other

What's a little roughhousing among friends? This Sloughi and his Golden Retriever pal practice a few wrestling moves.

sighthounds, Sloughis are sensitive to anesthetics, and your vet should be reminded of this. The normal lifespan of a well-cared-for Sloughi, living under proper conditions, is 12–16 years.

HEREDITARY HEALTH CONCERNS

All breeds of pure-bred dog can suffer from certain hereditary diseases. Breeders are well aware of these problems and work diligently to rid them from their lines of Sloughis. Discuss the following conditions with your chosen breeder. If the breeder has no interest or knowledge of these problems, find another breeder. A well-informed owner is the best owner for a Sloughi (or any other pure-bred dog), so it pays to be aware of these potential problems before adding a Sloughi to your life.

PROGRESSIVE RETINAL ATROPHY

Progressive retinal atrophy (PRA) is a hereditary blinding disorder found in most pure-bred dogs. PRA is a degenerative disease of the retina. The retina, a tissue located inside the back of the eye, contains specialized cells or photoreceptors that absorb the light focused on them by the lens. These photoreceptors convert the light into electrical nerve signals. The nerve signals from the retina are passed through the optic nerve to the brain, where they are

ABOVE: There's no telling where a Sloughi will find a comfortable place to rest. If the sunbeam happens to be across the kitchen table, the tall Sloughi has no problem climbing up to snooze in a warm spot. LEFT: The stoic Sloughi won't give away many hints that he's feeling under the weather. Look for clues such as lethargy and lack of interest in activity.

From desert to armchair! The Sloughi has adapted to life in the family home, and has also adjusted to making other canines part of his pack.

perceived as vision. The retinal photoreceptors are of two kinds: rods for night vision and cones for day and color vision.

PRA usually affects the rods first, leading to poor vision in darkness and twilight, and then affects the cones in later stages of the disease, when day vision also becomes impaired. As vision deteriorates, affected dogs adjust to their handicap by relying on their other senses (touch, hearing, smell) as long as their environment remains the same. As the disease progresses, the pupils of the eyes become noticeably very "shiny" and the lenses of the eyes

may become opaque, sometimes resulting in a cataract. In humans, a similar disorder is called retinitis pigmentosa.

Isolated cases of Sloughis becoming "early blind" have occurred occasionally during the past 25 years of breeding in Europe. However, not until 2000 was PRA properly diagnosed. At the same time, the genetic defect responsible for the disease was identified in the breed by a German team of scientists: Gabriele Dekomien, Maren Munte, Rene Gödde and Jörg Thomas Epplen of the Department of Molecular Human Genetics of

Ruhr University in Bochum, Germany.

The mode of inheritance and the age of onset of PRA vary tremendously from breed to breed. In the Sloughi, PRA has a late onset. Affected dogs appear normal when young but develop PRA as adults. From the few cases that are known, it seems that PRA starts around the age of two to three years and develops slowly over the following years. There are individual differences, and some Sloughis affected by PRA might develop the disease more quickly than others.

In the Sloughi, both dogs and bitches can inherit and pass on PRA to their offspring. It is inherited recessively in the Sloughi. Sloughis can be genotyped as being homozygous for the defective gene (PRA affected), heterozygous for the defective gene (carrier for PRA) or homozygous for the healthy gene (PRA clear).

PRA carriers and PRA-clear Sloughis are healthy and will never develop the disease. However, PRA carriers can pass on the disease to their offspring if they are bred to another carrier or a dog affected with PRA. Not many cases of PRA-affected Sloughis have been identified, but many dogs (at least one-third of the population) are carriers, so it is important to understand that the disease can be controlled only by genotyping for it.

Genotyping Sloughis for PRA is accomplished by sending blood samples to the Department of Molecular Human Genetics of Ruhr University in Bochum, Germany. In the US, the Sloughi Fanciers Association of America, OptiGen and the German team developed the same test for Sloughis in 2001. Now that the inheritance pattern of PRA in the Sloughi is well established, the *Deutscher Windhundzucht und Rennverband* in Germany and the Sloughi Fanciers Association of

A SENSORY HOUND
Although Sloughis are sighthounds that chase their prey on sight, they are also excellent trackers who can flush out game by scent before the final chase. They also have a very fine sense of hearing.

The Sloughi is a large, active and athletic sighthound who also enjoys some downtime and the comforts of home.

America (SFAA) have developed policies to control PRA in the breed. Registry in the SFAA stud book remains open to the offspring of two PRA-clear Sloughis, and to offspring of one carrier and one PRA-clear Sloughi. For each Sloughi used for breeding, documentation as to its PRA status needs to be provided. The DWZRV has a similar policy in Germany. When

looking for a Sloughi puppy, make sure that the breeder is genotyping his Sloughis for PRA and is registering his puppies in a stud book that requires genotyping for PRA in breeding animals.

HYPOTHYROIDISM

Hypothyroidism is another genetically inherited deficiency in the Sloughi. How exactly it is inherited is unclear, which makes it difficult to breed against, but the condition seems to run in families. Dogs who suffer from this low production of thyroid hormones should not be bred. Typically this condition shows up around five years of age. In one well-documented case known to the author, the Sloughi showed none of the typical signs of the condition (hair loss, for example) but started having seizures around the age of five years, which increased in severity between long intervals of several months. A test for thyroid hormones revealed low levels of T3 and T4. The dog was treated with tablets of thyroxin hormone each day and the seizures never occurred again. This case, however, met with some resistance from the vets in charge, as conventional veterinary medicine sees no connection between hypothyroidism and seizures. The causes for epilepsy can, of course, be very varied, and hypothyroidism is only one possibility.

Bitches with low thyroid levels have disturbed seasonal cycles. They too should not be bred, as their daughters will inherit this condition. Other hormonal imbalances are suspected of provoking the condition known as myocitic condition, in which the jaw muscles atrophy. In severe cases, animals cannot use their jaws to eat.

IMMUNE DEFICIENCIES AND ALLERGIES

Sloughis can also be affected by immune deficiencies of various kinds. They can also suffer from allergies to various foods (wheat, beef, potatoes, beets, peanuts, etc.), which can result in ear inflammation and infections. It is, however, difficult to pinpoint the genetic condition that may or may not underlie such conditions. In general, inbred dogs are more prone to such deficiencies.

CANCER

Cancer is the number-one killer of pure-bred dogs who die over the age of ten years. Various forms of cancer affect the Sloughi, such as mammary cancer in bitches, bone cancer and lymphoma. In such conditions, one does not really know for sure the respective roles of genetic predisposition versus an increasingly polluted environment whose toxicity constantly attacks the immune systems of people and animals alike.

A breed standard is a vital description of the ideal representative of a breed. Its purpose is to provide an ideal toward which every serious breeder aspires, and to provide consistency in the breed's correct type over time. This is why it is so important that standards, which are typically put together when the first specimens of a breed are presented to the fancy, should stay relatively conservative as time goes by. If a standard changes too often, so does the breed.

The standard gives the dog-show judge the description he needs to compare with the animal presented to him in the show ring. The original purpose of dog shows was to have one's own breeding stock evaluated by a judge who was knowledgeable about the breed. No two judges, however, interpret the standard in exactly the same way.

No dog is a perfect representation of the standard of the breed. This is why breeding is challenging and requires much patience and knowledge. The serious breeder raises good representatives of the breed by always breeding together two dogs who enhance each other in their quali-

ties and compensate for each other in their weaknesses. In each litter, there is usually a range of quality in the puppies, and a breeder with an eye for quality chooses the good-quality dogs for potential showing and possibly future breeding. It is the breeder's skill in selecting dogs to perpetuate the breed that leads generation after generation to improved specimens of the breed.

There are at this point in time three standards for the Sloughi breed. The standard of Europe's Fédération Cynologique Internationale (FCI) is the oldest. The standards of The Kennel Club in the UK and the United Kennel Club (UKC) in the US, both revised in 2002, are based on the FCI standard. The breed standard of the UKC is the most comprehensive and is presented here.

THE UNITED KENNEL CLUB STANDARD FOR THE SLOUGHI

HISTORY
The Sloughi is an ancient breed, developed in North Africa as the hunting sighthound of the Berbers, whose territory included Morocco, Algeria, Tunisia and

LEFT, TOP AND BOTTOM: A desert Sloughia with her pups. Note the brand on the mother's upper thigh. RIGHT: A Berber with a Sloughi in Tunisia. He is the breeder of all dogs on this page.

Libya. Sloughis have been used to hunt desert hare, desert fox, jackals and gazelles, as well as ostriches, wild boars and hyenas.

The first Sloughis arrived in Europe at the end of the 19th century, often with soldiers who had been stationed in North Africa and returned home with Sloughis. In 1935, the breed was officially recognized by the Fédération Cynologique Internationale. Because of the two World Wars, the breeding of Sloughis was interrupted and it was not resumed until the late 1960s after the war in Algeria.

In 1973, Mr. and Mrs. C. Rodarty imported the first Sloughi to the United States. Most Ameri-

can Sloughis are descended from Sloughis of French, Dutch and German breeding, which in turn descend from Sloughis imported from Morocco, Tunisia, Libya and Algeria. A few are direct imports from North Africa.

The Sloughi was recognized by the UKC in 1995.

GENERAL APPEARANCE
The Sloughi is a medium-sized sighthound, strong, lean and very racy. Its smooth-coated and long-legged body shows defined bony structure and lean muscles. Of squarish build, slightly higher than long, featherlight when moving, the Sloughi has a long wedge-shaped head, small drop

Photos taken by the author of (top left) a young Sloughi resting near a stable in Tunisia, (bottom left) a Kabylle dog, a shepherd breed that shares the same environment as the Sloughi in Tunisia and (right) a mountain Sloughi.

ears and a nearly straight topline from the base of the neck to the loin, where it arches very slightly and blends into a bony, sloping croup. The underline of the Sloughi is important to correct breed type. The brisket is deep but does not reach the elbow. The long sternum forms a straight line, parallel to the ground, which rises sharply into the tuck-up. The tail is long and carried low with an upward curve at the end. The atti-

tude is noble and somewhat aloof, and the expression of the large brown eyes gentle and melancholy.

Dogs are typically taller and more substantial than bitches, which should be smaller, more lightly built and feminine.

The Sloughi was treasured for its hunting skills, speed, agility and endurance over long distances. For this reason, it should give the general appearance of a short-coupled, well-balanced animal with no exaggeration of length of body or limbs, muscle development, nor curve of loin.

CHARACTERISTICS

The Sloughi is an intelligent and very driven hunter who chases on sight anything that moves, but also relies on olfactory and acoustic cues to chase prey. This "chasing on sight" behavior enables the Sloughi to be a competitive breed in non-commercial oval and straight racing events, as well as in lure coursing. It can also compete in open field hunts.

In Africa the Sloughi is an all-around working dog, used for hunting, but also as a watchdog.

For this reason the Sloughi is typically cautious with strangers, avoiding physical contact, but totally loyal, playful and affectionate with family. A Sloughi will however adjust to strangers if properly introduced by its owner.

The Sloughi does not respond well to harsh training. It does well, however, under a firm, consistent, fair and praising hand. *Faults:* Sharpness or shyness.

HEAD

In profile the head is long and refined but rather strong compared to other sighthounds. Seen from above, it has the shape of a long wedge, the skull being the widest part, tapering to the tip of the nose.

Skull: Seen from the side, the

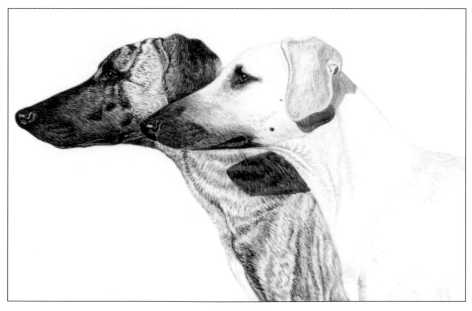

Typical Sloughi heads, painted by the author.

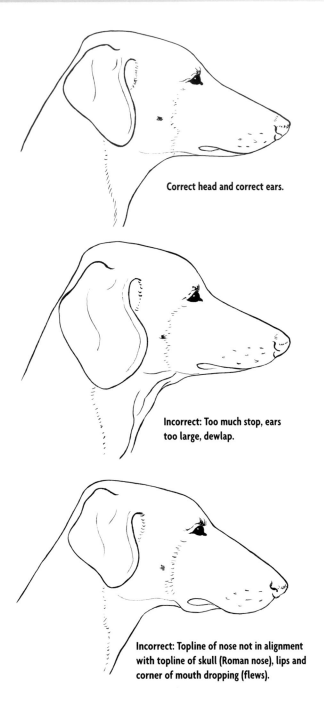

Correct head and correct ears.

Incorrect: Too much stop, ears too large, dewlap.

Incorrect: Topline of nose not in alignment with topline of skull (Roman nose), lips and corner of mouth dropping (flews).

top part of the skull is flat. The skull is rather broad, measuring approximately 4.7–5.5 inches (12–14 cm) between the ears. The skull is distinctly rounded at the back and curves harmoniously on the sides. The brows are scarcely projecting, the frontal groove is hardly marked, the stop is barely pronounced, and the occipital crest is barely visible. *Faults:* Skull too heavy and broad, too narrow, brows and stop too visible or insufficiently pronounced.

Muzzle: The muzzle has the shape of an elongated and moderately refined wedge and is roughly as long as the skull. The bridge of the nose is straight from its root. The nose leather, not being supported by the skeletal structure, bends slightly forward. The lips are thin and supple, just covering the lower jaw. The corner must be the least visible possible. *Faults:* Muzzle too short, too long, too wide, not in alignment with the top line of the skull, lips too strong and thick, corner of the mouth drooping. *Very serious fault:* Unpigmented areas on lips.

Nose: Black and strong, not pinched. *Faults:* Any color other than black. *Very serious fault:* Unpigmented areas on nose.

Teeth: Complete scissors bite. Teeth healthy and strong. Jaws strong and regular. Some Sloughis have additional pre-molars 1. *Faults:* Missing teeth, jaws too narrow. *Disqualifications:* Overshot or undershot.

Eyes: Large, dark, well set in their sockets, oval to almond-shaped and set somewhat obliquely. The expression is gentle, slightly sad and melancholy. The eye color is shades of dark brown to amber. The eye rims are pigmented. *Faults:* Eyes light amber, too small. *Very serious fault:* Unpigmented areas on eyelids.

Ears: The ears of the Sloughi are set high and drooping close to the head when the animal is at rest. The ears are of medium size, triangular in shape and slightly rounded at the tips. In movement or when the animal is nervous, the ears often fold backward. *Very serious faults:* Ears too long, tips hanging clearly below the lower jaw. *Disqualifications:* Ears erect or

Note the typical gentle expression of the Sloughi's dark eyes.

EAR CARRIAGE

The required ear carriage for the Sloughi has changed over the years. Ther earliest descriptions of the Sloughi from the 1850s–1930s described an ear larger than that of the Greyhound, but carried folded backwards in a similar fashion. The requirement for a lop ear hanging on both sides of the head is first exemplified in the 1938 French Sloughi standard. Today many Sloughis still occasionally fold their ears backwards when they are nervous or when they move.

with tips drooping forward, or small and folding backwards in a "rose ear."

NECK

The neck is long and springs well up from the shoulders. Its top line is slightly arched. The skin is fine, tight, with no dewlap and the hair is very smooth. *Faults:* Neck too short and thick, or too long and thin, dewlap.

The correct bite of the Sloughi.

A head shot of the Sloughi bitch Ch. Balsam Shi'Rayàn, showing correct shape and proportion of the head as seen from above.

BODY

A properly proportioned Sloughi is squarish to slightly higher than long. The following four lines drawn on the profile of a Sloughi form a square: From the withers down the back side of the front leg to the ground; from there to the front of the rear stifle; from there upward past the point of buttocks to the height at the withers; and from there, parallel to the ground, back to the withers.

The back is short, almost horizontal. In well-exercised animals, the withers are barely apparent. The topline is almost straight from the base of the neck, over the withers to the hips with a slight arch over the loin. The loin is short, lean, wide and slightly arched. The croup is bony and oblique with apparent hip bones.

The chest is not too wide. In depth, it hardly reaches the level of the elbow. In many Sloughis, it is about half an inch to an inch above the elbow. The body is well ribbed up. The ribs are flat, close fitting to a long, straight sternum. The floating ribs are more rounded. The under line first starts as a straight line (sternum) then rises up smoothly to a well tucked up belly. *Faults:* Croup too long, not bony enough, too round; topline not horizontal, saddle-back, rounded back, back too long, withers too apparent, chest not deep enough, too narrow or too wide, chest reaching below the elbow, round ribs (barrel chest), not enough tuck, abrupt underline. *Very serious faults:* A dog whose body is clearly longer than high or whose hip bones are clearly lower than the withers lacks breed type and should not be considered for champion points.

FOREQUARTERS

The shoulders are long and oblique, the arms are strong with good return of the upper arm. When properly angulated, the elbow will be in a direct vertical line below the uppermost tip of the shoulder blade. The shoulder blade and upper arm are of simi-lar length. The forelegs are

GAIT COMPARISON OF SIMILAR BREEDS

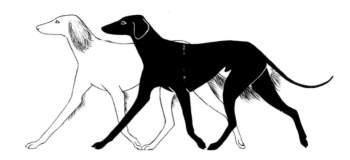

Gait of the Saluki.

Gait of the Sloughi.

Gait of the Azawakh.

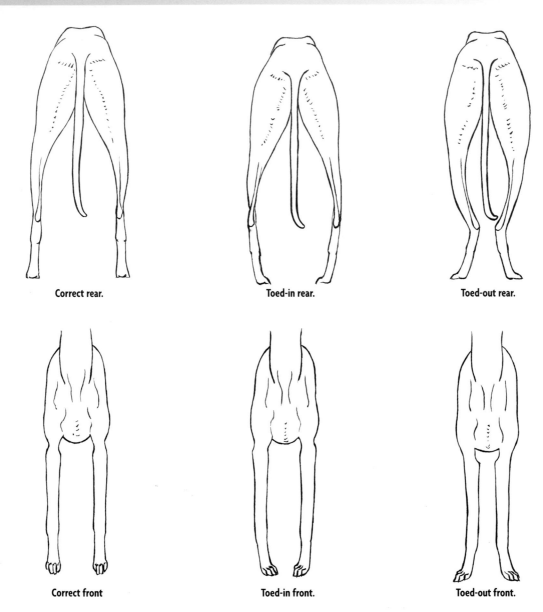

Correct rear.   **Toed-in rear.**   **Toed-out rear.**

Correct front   **Toed-in front.**   **Toed-out front.**

straight, bony and muscular. The pasterns are slightly sloping, supple and strong. The elbows are close to the body. *Faults:* Shoulders and upper arm too straight, pasterns too bent or too straight, legs not parallel to each other, toes turned in or out.

One of the top winning Sloughis in the USA, Ch. Bassel Shi'Rayân, a red black brindle.

All-time top-winning bitch in the USA, World Winner 1997, FCI Int. Ch. A'ssissa Shi'Rayân, a sand brindle black mask.

This sand black mask bitch is a top-winning Sloughia of British breeding. Falconcrag Zouala took Best of Breed at Crufts in 2002 and was the number-one Sloughi in England for 2001-2002.

World Winner dog 1997, FCI Int. Ch. Batal Shi'Rayân, a red brindle.

HINDQUARTERS

The thigh is lean, flat and muscular. The second thigh is long and well muscled. Hocks are strong and well bent. The rear pasterns are strong and have no dewclaws. The hindlegs are moderately angulated. The tendons are well chiseled. *Faults:* Bulging round muscles, not enough or too much angulation, legs not parallel to each other, toes turned in or out.

Ch. Batal Shi-Rayân.

Tarfa, a Tunisian import into the US.

Ch. Assissa Shi'Rayân and Ch. El Emin Schuru-esch-Schams showing the difference in size between a bitch and a dog.

FEET

The feet are lean and have the shape of an elongated oval. In many lightly built Sloughis, the foot is shaped like a hare-foot. The nails are black or just pigmented. *Faults:* Feet flat, toes not tight, toes turned in or out.

TAIL

The tail is long, thin and set in line with the croup, carried low with a typical upward curve in the resting position. The tail should be long enough to reach the point of the hocks. When the Sloughi trots, the tail should be carried below the horizontal line of the back. *Faults:* Tail too short, coarse, with too much hair and too thick, badly carried.

COAT

The coat of the Sloughi is always smooth. It is short, tight and fine all over the body. The Sloughi is presented in natural condition and any tampering with its looks should be strongly discouraged. *Faults:* Coat hard and coarse. *Disqualifications:* Coat too long and feathering on the tail and/or legs.

COLOR

The coat colors of the Sloughi are all shades of light sand (cream) to mahogany red fawn, with or without black markings such as brindling, black mask, black ears, dark overlay and black mantle, with no invasive white markings. The darkest coats are red black brindle and red brindle with black mask and black mantle. A white patch on the chest and a few white hairs at the tip of the toes, difficult to detect on light coats, should be tolerated in otherwise outstanding specimens with darker coats. *Faults:* Large white patch on the chest. *Disqualifications:* Color not in accordance with the standard. Extensive white markings such as parti-color, white socks and white blaze. Albinism.

The all-time top-winning multiple-Best-in-Show American Sloughi, FCI Int. Ch. Aswad Shi'Rayân.

HEIGHT AND WEIGHT

For mature males, height at the withers ranges between 26.4–28.3 inches (66–72 cm), with the ideal size being 27.6 inches (70 cm). Weight ranges between 55 and 65 pounds. For mature females, height at the withers ranges between 24–26.7 inches (61–68 cm), with the ideal size being 25.6 inches (65 cm). Weight ranges between 45 and 50 pounds.

GAIT

The Sloughi has a smooth, featherlight, floating and effortless gait, tail held low, head at a moderate angle to the body. As a result of the squarish build and moderate angulations, there is no exaggeration in extension. The front paw does not reach beyond the tip of the nose. The racing style resembles that of the Greyhound but, because of its straighter topline, the Sloughi

Aswad and his brother Amir, both top racers in the US.

The outline of a Sloughi's gait, demonstrated by an outstanding specimen of the breed.

cannot flex its back as much as the Greyhound. *Faults:* Hackney gait, gait restricted, uneven and loose, not covering enough ground.

DISQUALIFICATIONS
Unilateral or bilateral cryptorchid. Viciousness or extreme shyness. Overshot or undershot. Ears erect or with tips drooping forward, or small and folding backwards in a "rose ear." Coat too long and feathering on the tail and/or legs. Color not in accordance with the standard. Extensive white markings such as parti-color, white socks and white blaze. Albinism.

DESERT VS. MOUNTAIN TYPE
There are two different kinds of Sloughis, the "desert" Sloughi, finer boned and smaller than the "mountain" Sloughi. However both have otherwise identical features, and both can be found in the same litter.

FROM LEFT TO RIGHT: Sand black mask, sand brindle black mask, red brindle and black brindle. Ch. Aswad and his three sons, Fa'iq, Batal and Bassel Shi'Rayàn.

BELOW, FROM LEFT TO RIGHT: Golden brindle, sand black mask, sand black mask overlay, sand brindle black mask, red brindle, red black mask, sand brindle black mask and sand black mask. Compare in size the bitches (numbers 1, 2, 3, 4 and 6 in line) and the males (numbers 5, 7 and 8).

SLOUGHI

Before deciding that you will begin your search for a Sloughi puppy, it is essential that you are fully clear in your mind that this is absolutely the most suitable breed for you and for your family. There is no disputing the fact that this is a very special breed, and all the pros and cons must be carefully weighed against each other before reaching the important decision that a Sloughi is going to enter your life.

Once you have made that decision, you must also ask yourself why you want a Sloughi, as a pet, as a competition dog or as a show dog. This should be made clear to the breeder when you make your initial inquiries, for you will certainly need to take the breeder's advice as which available puppy displays the most promise for the show ring. If looking for a pet, you should discuss your family and living situation with the breeder, and again take his advice as to which puppy is likely to suit you best. Another consideration, of course, is whether you prefer the mountain-type or the desert-type Sloughi. This will guide your selection of a breeder.

You should have done plenty of research on the breed and preferably have visited a few breed-club or rare-breed shows at which the Sloughi is entered, giving you an opportunity to see the breed in some numbers. Visiting shows also provides you with the chance to see the dogs with their breeders and owners, so you can watch them interacting and also give thought to which people's stock you like best. Shows are wonderful for meeting Sloughi people and making contacts in the breed, provided you approach them when they are not busy with their dogs.

THE NEWBORN PUPPY

As other dog breeds, the ears and eyes of Sloughi puppies are closed during the first two weeks after birth. Puppies use their senses of smell and touch to stay together and to find the source of milk, as they can neither see nor hear.

Two days old.

Once you have selected a breeder and have the opportunity to visit a litter, watch the puppies interact together. See which little personality appeals to you most, obviously also taking into account the overall quality of the dog, especially if destined for a show home. Never be tempted to take pity on an unduly shy puppy, for in doing so you will be asking for trouble in the long run; such a dog is likely to encounter problems in socializing.

Remember that the dog you select should remain with you for the duration of his life, which is usually around 12 to 16 years, so making the right decision from the outset is of utmost importance. The Sloughi bonds closely with his one owner (and family) and often does not transfer to a new home very easily.

Puppies almost invariably look enchanting, but you must select one from a caring breeder who has given the puppies all the attention they deserve and has looked after them well. It is important for breeders to socialize puppies as early as possible, and it should be apparent when you meet the litter that this has been done.

Appearance-wise, the puppy you select should look well fed, but not pot-bellied, as this might indicate worms. Eyes should look bright and clear, without discharge. The nose should be moist, an indication of good health, but should never be runny; it goes without saying that there should certainly be no evidence of loose bowels or parasites. The puppy you choose should also have a healthy-looking coat, an important indicator of good health internally.

Something else to consider is whether or not to take out veteri-

Is there anything more beautiful than you and your Sloughi becoming part of the same pack? Sloughis are good pets and great friends.

MAKE A COMMITMENT

Dogs are most assuredly man's best friend, but they are also a lot of work. When you add a Sloughi puppy to your family, you also are adding to your daily responsibilities for well over a decade. Dogs need more than just food, water and a place to sleep. They also require training (which will be ongoing throughout the lifetime of the dog), activity to keep them physically and mentally fit and hands-on attention every day, plus grooming and healthcare. Your life as you now know it may well disappear. Are you prepared for such drastic changes?

needed. How much of your dog's care is covered by insurance will depend on the extent of the policy you take out; many options now are available, as veterinary insurance is becoming more popular.

A COMMITTED NEW OWNER
By now you should understand what makes the Sloughi a most unique and special dog, and you should be sure that the breed will fit nicely into your family and lifestyle. If you have researched breeders, you should be able to recognize a knowledgeable and responsible Sloughi breeder who cares not only about his pups but also about what kind of owner you will be. If you have completed the final step in your new journey, you have found a litter, or possibly even two, of quality Sloughi pups, keeping in mind that the search for these rare-breed pups will take time.

A visit with the puppies and their breeder should be an education in itself. Breed research, breeder selection and puppy visitation are very important aspects of finding the puppy of your dreams. Beyond that, these things also lay the foundation for a successful future with your pup. Puppy personalities within each litter vary, from the shy and easy-going puppy to the one who is dominant and assertive, with most pups falling somewhere in between. By spending time with

nary insurance. Vet's bills can mount up, and you must always be certain that sufficient funds are available to give your dog any veterinary attention that may be

the puppies, you will be able to recognize certain behaviors and what these behaviors indicate about each pup's temperament. Which type of pup will complement your family dynamics is best determined by observing the puppies in action within their "pack." Your breeder's expertise and recommendations are very valuable. Although you may fall in love with a bold and brassy male, the breeder may suggest that another pup would be best for you. The breeder's experience in rearing Sloughi pups and matching their temperaments with appropriate humans offers the best assurance that your pup will meet your needs and expectations. The type of puppy that you select is just as important as your decision that the Sloughi is the breed for you.

The decision to live with a Sloughi is a serious commitment and not one to be taken lightly. This puppy is a living sentient being that will be dependent on you for basic survival for his entire life. Beyond the basics of survival—food, water, shelter and protection—he needs much, much more. The new pup needs love, nurturing and a proper canine education to mold him into a responsible, well-behaved canine citizen. Your Sloughi's health and good manners will need consistent monitoring and regular "tune-ups." So your job as a responsible

dog owner will be ongoing throughout every stage of his life. If you are not prepared to accept these responsibilities and commit to them for the next decade, likely longer, then you are not prepared to own a dog of any breed.

Although the responsibilities of owning a dog may at times tax your patience, the joy of living with your Sloughi far outweighs the workload, and a well-mannered adult dog is worth your time and effort. Before your very

PROUD PARENTS
Sloughias are great mothers and, under proper conditions, most will continue feeding their puppies until about eight to ten weeks of age. Some will switch to regurgitating food for their puppies, when their milk dries up. Some male Sloughis love puppies and act as puppy guards when around them.

A litter of Sloughis at one week of age with their eyes still closed.

A pair of Sloughi puppies at six weeks of age.

Sloughi puppies at two months of age.

Sloughi puppies at three months of age.

eyes, your new charge will grow up to be your most loyal friend, devoted to you unconditionally.

YOUR SLOUGHI SHOPPING LIST

Just as expectant parents prepare a nursery for their baby, so should you ready your home for the arrival of your Sloughi pup. If you have the necessary puppy supplies purchased and in place before he comes home, it will ease the puppy's transition from the warmth and familiarity of his mom and littermates to the brand-new environment of his new home and human family. You will be too busy to stock up and

prepare your house after your pup comes home, that's for sure! Imagine how a pup must feel upon being transported to a strange new place. It's up to you to comfort him and to let your little pup know that he is going to be happy with you.

FOOD AND WATER BOWLS

Your puppy will need separate bowls for his food and water. Stainless steel pans are generally preferred to plastic bowls, since they sterilize better and pups are less inclined to chew on the metal. Heavy-duty ceramic bowls are popular, but consider how often you will have to pick up those heavy bowls! Buy adult-sized food and water bowls, as your puppy will grow into them before you know it.

CRATE

To someone unfamiliar with the use of crates in dog training, it may seem like punishment to shut a dog in a crate, but this is not the case at all. Although not all breeders advocate crate training, many breeders and trainers are recommending crates as preferred tools for show puppies and pet puppies alike. Crates are not cruel—crates have many humane and highly effective uses in dog care and training. For example, crate training is a very popular and very successful house-training method. A crate can keep your dog safe

The wire crate is popular for use in the home, as it provides safe confinement with open wire construction on all sides, allowing the dog to feel part of his surroundings.

PHOTO BY PAULETTE BRAUN

during travel and, perhaps most importantly, a crate provides your dog with a place of his own in your home. It serves as a "doggie bedroom" of sorts—your Sloughi can curl up in his crate when he wants to sleep or when he just needs a break. Many dogs sleep in their crates overnight. With soft bedding and his favorite toy, a crate becomes a cozy pseudo-den for your dog. Like his ancestors, he too will seek out the comfort and retreat of a den—you just happen to be providing him with something a little more luxurious than what his early ancestors enjoyed. Keep in mind that the Sloughi does not relish being confined in his crate for more than a few hours at a time.

As far as purchasing a crate, the type that you buy is up to you. It will most likely be one of the two most popular types: wire or fiberglass. There are advantages and disadvantages to each type. For example, a wire crate is more open, allowing the air to flow through and affording the dog a view of what is going on around

him, while a fiberglass crate is sturdier. Both can double as travel crates, providing protection for the dog in the car.

The size of the crate is another thing to consider. Puppies do not stay puppies forever—in fact, sometimes it seems as if they grow right before your eyes. A small crate may be fine for a very young Sloughi pup, but it will not do him much good for long! Unless you have the money and

Stands at dog shows offer many products for the dog owner and fancier, from necessities to novelties.

Your local pet shop will have an assortment of food and water bowls. As your Sloughi grows taller, the vet may suggest that elevating your dog's bowls is better for his digestion, although there is some debate over this feeding method.

TOYS 'R SAFE

The vast array of tantalizing puppy toys is staggering. Stroll through any pet shop or pet-supply outlet and you will see that the choices can be overwhelming. However, not all dog toys are safe or sensible. Most very young puppies enjoy soft woolly toys that they can snuggle with and carry around. (You know they have outgrown them when they shred them up!) Avoid toys that have buttons, tabs or other enhancements that can be chewed off and swallowed. Soft toys that squeak are fun, but make sure your puppy does not disembowel the toy and remove (and swallow) the squeaker. Toys that rattle or make noise can excite a puppy, but they present the same danger as the squeaky kind and so require supervision. Hard rubber toys that bounce can also entertain a pup, but make sure the size of the toy is correct for your Sloughi.

sized crate will be necessary for a full-grown Sloughi, who can stand between 24 and a little over 28 inches high at the withers.

BEDDING AND CRATE PADS

Your puppy will enjoy some type of soft bedding in his crate, something he can snuggle into and feel cozy and secure when crated. Old towels or blankets are good choices for a young pup, since he may (and probably will) have a toileting accident or two in the crate or decide to chew on the bedding material. Once he is fully trained and out of the early chewing stage, you can replace the puppy bedding with a permanent crate pad if you prefer. Crate pads and other dog beds run the gamut from inexpensive to high-end doggie-designer styles, but don't splurge on the good stuff until you are sure that your puppy is reliable and won't tear it up or make a puddle on it.

PUPPY TOYS

Just as infants and older children require objects to stimulate their minds and bodies, puppies need toys to entertain their curious brains, wiggly paws and achy teeth. A fun array of safe doggie toys will help satisfy your puppy's chewing instincts and distract him from gnawing on the leg of your antique chair or your new leather sofa. Most puppy toys are cute and look as if they would

the inclination to buy a new crate every time your pup has a growth spurt, it is better to get one that will accommodate your dog both as a pup and at full size. A giant-

be a lot of fun, but not all are necessarily safe or good for your puppy, so use caution when you go puppy-toy shopping.

Although Sloughis are not known to be voracious chewers like many other dogs, they still appreciate the art of chewing. The best "chewcifiers" are nylon and hard rubber bones which are safe to gnaw on and come in sizes appropriate for all age groups and breeds. Be especially careful of natural bones, which can splinter or develop dangerous sharp edges; pups can easily swallow or choke on those bone splinters. Veterinarians often tell of surgical nightmares involving bits of splintered bone, because in addition to the danger of choking, the sharp pieces can damage the intestinal tract.

Similarly, rawhide chews, while a favorite of most dogs and puppies, can be equally dangerous. Pieces of rawhide are easily swallowed after they get soft and gummy from chewing, and dogs have been known to choke on large pieces of ingested rawhide. Rawhide chews should be offered only when you can supervise the puppy.

Soft woolly toys are special puppy favorites. They come in a wide variety of cute shapes and sizes; some look like little stuffed animals. Puppies love to shake them up and toss them about, or simply carry them around. Be

careful of fuzzy toys that have button eyes or noses that your pup could chew off and swallow, and make sure that he does not "disembowel" a squeaky toy to remove the squeaker. Braided rope toys are similar in that they are fun to chew and toss around, but they shred easily and the strings are easy to swallow. The strings are not digestible and, if the

COST OF OWNERSHIP
The purchase price of your puppy is merely the first expense in the typical dog budget. Quality dog food, veterinary care (for illness and for health maintenance) and all sorts of dog supplies will add up to big bucks every year. Can you adequately afford to support a canine addition to the family?

COLLARING OUR CANINES

The standard flat collar with a buckle or a snap, in leather, nylon or cotton, is widely regarded as the everyday all-purpose collar. If the collar fits correctly, you should be able to fit two fingers between the collar and the dog's neck. Such a flat collar is suitable for most breeds of dog, but sighthound breeds (with slender skulls and necks) and can easily back out of this type of collar.

Leather Buckle Collars

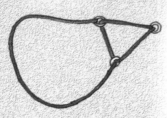

Limited-Slip Collar

The martingale, Greyhound or limited-slip collar is preferred by many dog owners and trainers. It is fixed with an extra loop that tightens when pressure is applied to the leash. The martingale collar gets tighter but does not "choke" the dog. The limited-slip collar should only be used for walking and training, not for free play or interaction with another dog. These types of collar should never be left on the dog, as the extra loop can lead to accidents.

Choke collars, usually made of stainless steel, are made for training purposes, but are not recommended for small dogs or heavily coated breeds. The chains can injure small dogs or damage long/abundant coats. Thin nylon choke leads are commonly used on show dogs while in the ring, though they are not practical for everyday use.

The harness, with two or three straps that attach over the dog's shoulders and around his torso, is a humane and safe alternative to the conventional collar. By and large, a well-made harness is virtually escape-proof. Harnesses are available in nylon and mesh and can be outfitted on most dogs, with chest girths ranging from 10 to 30 inches.

Snap Bolt Choke Collar

Harness

Nylon Collar

Quick-Click Closure

Snake Chain

Chrome Steel

Fur-Saver

Choke Chain Collars

A head collar, composed of a nylon strap that goes around the dog's muzzle and a second strap that wraps around his neck, offers the owner better control over his dog. This device is recommended for problem-solving with dogs (including jumping up, pulling and aggressive behaviors), but must be used with care.

A training halter, including a flat collar and two straps, made of nylon and webbing, is designed for walking. There are several on the market; some are more difficult to put on the dog than others. The halter harness, with two small slip rings at each end, is recommended for ease of use.

puppy doesn't pass them in his stool, he could end up at the vet's office. As with rawhides, your puppy should be closely monitored with soft and rope toys.

If you believe that your pup has ingested one of these forbidden objects, check his stools for the next couple of days to see if he passes them when he defecates. At the same time, also watch for signs of intestinal distress. A call to your veterinarian might be in order to get his advice and be on the safe side.

An all-time favorite toy for puppies (young and old) is the empty gallon milk jug. Hard plastic juice containers—46 ounces or more—are also excellent. Such containers make lots of noise when they are batted about and puppies go crazy with delight as they play with them. However, they don't often last very long, so be sure to remove and replace them when they get chewed up.

A word of caution about homemade toys: be careful with your choices of non-traditional play objects. Never use old shoes or socks, since a puppy cannot distinguish between the old ones on which he's allowed to chew and the new ones in your closet that are strictly off-limits. This principle applies to anything that resembles something that you don't want your puppy to chew up.

Some owners like to dress their adult Sloughis in decorative collars, befitting the breed's noble heritage.

COLLARS

A lightweight nylon collar is the best choice for a very young pup. Quick-clip collars are easy to put on and remove, and they can be adjusted as the puppy grows. Introduce him to his collar as soon as he comes home to get him accustomed to wearing it. He'll get used to it quickly and won't mind a bit. Make sure that it is snug enough that it won't slip off, yet loose enough to be comfortable for the pup. You should be able to slip two fingers between the collar and his neck. Check the collar often, as puppies grow in spurts and his collar can become too tight almost overnight. Choke collars are for training purposes only and should never be used on a puppy under four or five months old. The chain-type choke collars are not recommended for the Sloughi.

LEASHES

A 6-foot nylon lead is an excellent choice for a young puppy. It is lightweight and not as tempting to chew as a leather lead. You can switch to a 6-foot leather lead after your pup has grown and is used to walking politely on a lead. For initial puppy walks and house-training purposes, you should invest in a shorter lead so that you have more control over the puppy. At first, you don't want him wandering too far away from you; plus, when taking him out for toileting, you will want to keep him in the specific area

chosen for his potty spot.

Once the puppy is heel-trained with a traditional leash, you can consider purchasing a retractable lead. A flexible lead is excellent for walking adult dogs that are already leash-wise. The "flexi" allows the dog to roam farther away from you and explore a wider area when out walking, and also retracts when you need to keep him close to you.

HOME SAFETY FOR YOUR PUPPY

The importance of puppy-proofing cannot be overstated. In addition to making your house comfortable for your Sloughi's arrival, you also must make sure that your house is safe for your puppy before you bring him home. There are countless hazards in the owner's personal living environment that a pup can sniff, chew, swallow or destroy. Many are obvious; others are not. Do a thorough advance house check to remove or rearrange those things that could hurt your puppy, keeping any potentially dangerous items out of areas to which he will have access.

Electrical cords are especially dangerous, since puppies view them as irresistible chew toys. Unplug and remove all exposed cords or fasten them beneath a baseboard where the puppy cannot reach them. Veterinarians

> ## TOXIC PLANTS
> Plants are natural puppy magnets and many can be harmful, even fatal, if ingested by a puppy or adult dog. Scout your yard and home interior and remove any plants, bushes or flowers that could be even mildly dangerous. It could save your puppy's life. You can obtain a complete list of toxic plants from your veterinarian, at the public library or by looking online.

and firefighters can tell you horror stories about electrical burns and house fires that resulted from puppy-chewed electrical cords. Consider this a most serious precaution for your puppy and the rest of your family.

Scout your home for tiny objects that might be seen at a pup's eye level. Keep medication bottles and cleaning supplies well out of reach, and do the same with waste baskets and other trash containers. It goes without saying that you should not use rodent poison or other toxic chemicals in any area in which the pup may roam, and that you must keep such containers safely locked up. You will be amazed at how many places a curious puppy can discover!

Once your house has cleared inspection, check your yard. A sturdy fence, well embedded into the ground, will give your dog a safe place to play and potty. Sloughis are known to dig trenches and caves and be able to clear a 6-foot fence with nothing more than a running start. The remedy is to make the fence embedded deeply into the ground and high enough so that it really is impossible for your dog to get over it (about 8 feet should suffice). Check the fence periodically for necessary repairs. If there is a weak link or space to squeeze through, you can be sure a determined Sloughi will discover it.

ASK THE VET

Help your vet help you become a well-informed dog owner. Don't be shy about becoming involved in your puppy's veterinary care by asking questions and gaining as much knowledge as you can. For starters, ask what shots your puppy is getting and what diseases they prevent, and discuss with your vet the safest way to vaccinate, as the Sloughi is sensitive to inoculations. Find out what is involved in your dog's annual wellness visits. If you plan to spay or neuter, discuss the best age at which to have this done. Start out on the right "paw" with your puppy's vet and develop good communication with him, as he will care for your dog's health throughout the dog's entire life.

The garage and shed can be hazardous places for a pup, as things like fertilizers, chemicals and tools are usually kept there. It's best to keep these areas off-limits to the pup. Antifreeze is especially dangerous to dogs, as they find the taste appealing and it only takes a few licks from the driveway to kill a dog, puppy or adult, small breed or large.

VISITING THE VETERINARIAN
A good veterinarian is your Sloughi puppy's best health-insurance policy. If you do not already have a vet, ask your breeder, friends and experienced dog

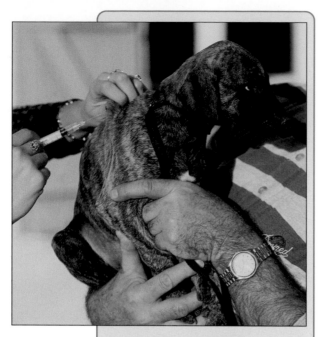

VACCINATION DEBATE

Vaccinations are recommended for all puppies by the American Veterinary Medical Association (AVMA). Some vaccines are absolutely necessary, while others depend upon a dog's or puppy's individual exposure to certain diseases or the animal's immune history. According to the law, rabies vaccinations are required in all 50 states. Some diseases are fatal while others are treatable, making the need for vaccinating against the latter questionable. Follow your vet's recommendations to keep your dog fully immunized and protected in the safest way, as sighthounds can be sensitive to injections. You can also review the AVMA directive on vaccinations at www.avma.org.

people in your area for recommendations so that you can select a good vet before you bring your Sloughi puppy home. Also arrange for your puppy's first veterinary examination beforehand, since your puppy should visit the vet within a day or so of coming home. Some sellers' contracts indicate that you only have 10 to 14 days to return the puppy for a congenital problem, an infectious disease or the like.

It's important to make sure your puppy's first visit to the vet is a pleasant and positive one. The vet should take great care to befriend the pup and handle him gently to make their first meeting a positive experience. The vet will give the pup a thorough physical examination and set up a schedule for vaccinations and other necessary wellness visits. Be sure to show your vet any health and inoculation records, which you should have received from your breeder. Your vet is a great source of canine health information, so be sure to ask questions and take notes. Creating a health journal for your puppy will make a handy reference for his wellness as well as any future health problems that may arise.

MEETING THE FAMILY

Your Sloughi's homecoming is an exciting time for all members of the family, and it's only natural that everyone will be eager to meet him, pet him and play with him. However, for the puppy's sake, it's best to make these initial family meetings as uneventful as possible so that the pup is not overwhelmed with too much too soon. Remember, he has just left his dam and his littermates and is away from the breeder's home for the first time. Despite his wagging tail, he is still apprehensive and wondering where he is and who all these strange humans are. It's best to let him explore on his own and meet the family members as he feels comfortable. Let him investigate all the new smells, sights and sounds at his own pace. Children should be especially careful to not get overly excited, use loud voices or hug the pup too tightly. Be calm, gentle and affectionate, and be ready to comfort him if he appears frightened or uneasy.

Be sure to show your puppy his new crate during this first day home. Toss a treat or two inside the crate; if he associates the crate with food, he will associate the crate with good things. If he is comfortable with the crate, you can offer him his first meal inside it. Leave the door ajar so he can wander in and out as he chooses.

FIRST NIGHT IN HIS NEW HOME

So much has happened in your Sloughi puppy's first day away from the breeder. He's had his first car ride to his new home. He's met

Where there's a puppy, there are puppy teeth that a responsible owner must keep occupied with proper safe chewing.

his new human family and perhaps the other family pets. He has explored his new house and yard, at least those places where he is to be allowed during his first weeks at home. He may have visited his new veterinarian. He has eaten his first meal or two away from his dam and litter-mates. Surely that's enough to tire out an eight-week-old Sloughi pup...or so you hope!

It's bedtime. During the day, the pup investigated his crate, which is his new den and sleep-ing space, so it is not entirely strange to him. Line the crate with a soft towel or blanket that he can snuggle into and gently place him in the crate for the night. Some breeders send home a piece of bedding from where the pup slept with his littermates, and those familiar scents are a great comfort for the puppy on his first night without his siblings.

He will probably whine or cry. The puppy is objecting to the confinement and the fact that he is alone for the first time. This can be a stressful time for you as well as for the pup. It's important that you remain strong and don't let the puppy out of his crate to comfort him. He will fall asleep eventually. If you release him, the puppy will learn that crying means "out" and will continue that habit. You are laying the groundwork for future habits. Some breeders find that soft

music can soothe a crying pup and help him get to sleep.

SOCIALIZING YOUR PUPPY
The next 20 weeks of your Sloughi puppy's life are the most important of his entire lifetime. A properly socialized puppy will grow up to be a confident and stable adult who will be a plea-sure to live with and a welcome addition to the neighborhood. The importance of socialization cannot be overemphasized. Research on canine behavior has proven that puppies who are not exposed to new sights, sounds, people and animals during their first 20 weeks of life will grow up to be timid and fearful, even aggressive, and unable to flourish outside their home environment

Socializing your puppy is not difficult and, in fact, will be a fun time for you both. Lead training goes hand in hand with socializa-tion, so your puppy will be learn-ing how to walk on a lead at the same time that he's meeting the neighborhood. Because the Sloughi is a such a fascinating breed, people will naturally be drawn to him and will want to meet him. Take him for short walks, to the park and to other dog-friendly places where he will encounter new people. Just make sure that you supervise these meetings, keeping in mind that the Sloughi does not usually take to strangers right away and will need time to warm up to new people. Also be sure that any children you meet are polite and careful with your pup. A bad experience in puppyhood can impact a dog for life, so a pup that has a negative experience with a child may grow up to be shy or even aggressive around children.

Take your puppy along on your daily errands. Puppies are natural "people magnets" and most people who see your pup will want to pet him. Supervised encounters with friendly people will help to mold him into a confident adult dog. Likewise, you will soon feel like a confident, responsible dog owner, rightly proud of your handsome Sloughi.

Be especially careful of your puppy's encounters and experiences during the eight-to-ten-week-old period, which is also called the "fear period." This is a serious imprinting period and all contact during this time should be gentle and positive. A frightening or negative event could leave a permanent impression that could affect his future behavior if a similar situation arises.

Also make sure that your puppy has received his first and second rounds of vaccinations before you expose him to other dogs or bring him to places that other dogs may frequent. Avoid dog parks and other strange-dog areas until your vet assures you that your puppy is fully immunized and

THE CRITICAL SOCIALIZATION PERIOD

Canine research has shown that a puppy's 8th through 16th week is the most critical learning period of his life. This is when the puppy "learns to learn," a time when he needs positive experiences to build confidence and stability. Puppies who are not exposed to different people and situations outside the home during this period can grow up to be fearful and sometimes aggressive. This is also the best time for puppy lessons, since he has not yet acquired any bad habits that could undermine his ability to learn.

resistant to the diseases that can be passed between canines. Discuss safe socialization with your breeder, as some breeders recommend socializing the puppy even before he has received all of his inoculations.

PROPER CARE OF YOUR

SLOUGHI

FEEDING YOUR SLOUGHI
Let's keep in mind that the Sloughi is a breed that was raised for centuries in an environment that typically did not provide for very rich foods. In North Africa, Sloughi puppies are raised on bread dipped in goat milk, and adults on couscous, leftovers, an egg yolk here and there and dates. For this reason, Sloughis do not do well on rich or high-protein foods. They also do not do too well on the same food every day, as they become bored easily.

They are a variety of types of commercial kibble on the market. For your Sloughi, the best is to choose one with not more than 20–25% protein for your adult, and 25% for your puppy. Avoid foods that are very salty, which will make the dog drink more, resulting in difficulty in house-training. Choose foods with whole chicken, lamb or beef, and vegetables if possible, and preserved with natural ingredients. Several of the commercial companies offer various flavors within their brands. Alternating between these various kinds will help keep your Sloughi

interested in his food. As your Sloughi ages, you might try one of the foods designed for older, less active dogs.

An alternative to commercial food is to feed your Sloughi a natural diet consisting of fresh meat, vegetables, fruit, yogurt, cottage cheese and egg yolks as well as noodles, rice or cereals. This type of feeding requires more effort on your part, as well as a good knowledge of nutrition, but is fun to prepare if you like cooking.

A good way to ensure the best feeding for your Sloughi is to feed some commercial food and some natural food separately. Supplements in the form of vitamin and Brewer's yeast tablets or powdered kelp, liquid cod liver oil and the like can be added at intervals and in moderation, particularly in growing dogs. Ask your breeder or vet about appropriate dosages.

We find that the best time of the day for the main meal is in the late afternoon for the adult dog, with a few dog biscuits at breakfast. For the puppy, the two main meals would be in the morning and the late afternoon, with a snack at noon, such as a bowl of milk. Sloughis, unless they are spayed or neutered, do not tend to become overweight, eating only what they need. Of course, the more often you feed during the day, the more often the dog will have to go out to relieve himself. A regular feeding schedule ensures a regular "potty rhythm" with obvious house-training advantages.

Lastly, keep in mind that you should be careful what human foods you offer to your Sloughi. Do not give him sweet treats, candy or chocolate, which is notoriously toxic to dogs.

WATER
Just as your dog needs proper nutrition from his food, water is an essential nutrient as well.

Water keeps the dog's body properly hydrated and promotes normal function of the body's systems. During house-training, it is necessary to keep an eye on how much water your Sloughi is drinking, but once he is reliably trained he should have access to clean fresh water at all times, especially if you feed dry food. Make certain that the dog's water bowl is clean, and change the water often.

A word of caution concerning your deep-chested Sloughi's water intake: he should never be allowed to gulp water, especially at mealtimes. In fact, his water intake should be limited at mealtimes as a rule. This simple daily precaution can go a long way in protecting your dog from the dangerous and potentially fatal gastric torsion (bloat).

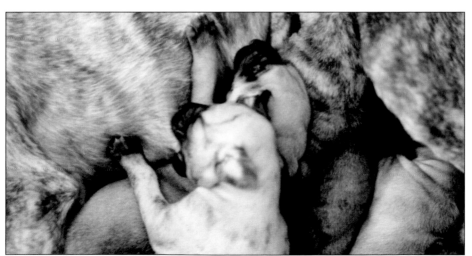

Sloughi puppies one day old, nursing. There is no better food for puppies than their mother's milk.

EXERCISE

The Sloughi is a highly active dog, so exercise is necessary for his health, happiness and mental stimulation. Daily exercise is important, and most Sloughis will accept as much as they are given. While lead work is important, it is essential that some of the daily exercise program gives the hound an opportunity to run free (in an enclosed area) so as to stretch his limbs, as well as to release pent-up energy. After exercise, the dog should be allowed to settle down quietly for a rest. Remember that, following exercise, at least one full hour should always be allowed before feeding; likewise, dogs should wait at least an hour after mealtimes before exercising. Puppies should have only limited exercise during their crucial period of bone growth, so young dogs should be exercised with care.

Because Sloughis are

> **TWO'S COMPANY**
> One surefire method of increasing your adult dog's exercise plan is to adopt a second dog. If your dog is well socialized, he should take to his new canine pal in no time and soon the two will be giving each other lots of activity and exercise as they play, romp and explore together. Most owners agree that two dogs is hardly much more work than one. If you cannot afford a second dog, get together with a friend or neighbor who has a well-trained dog. Your dog will definitely enjoy the company of a new four-legged playmate.

accomplished escapologists, it goes without saying that the yard and run areas must be completely dog-proof, and the perimeters must be checked regularly to be sure that the Sloughi is not working on a new exit route! This would most likely be by means of digging under a fence, but remember that a Sloughi can clear a 6-foot fence, so "over" is as important as "under" when securing your yard.

GROOMING

ROUTINE MAINTENANCE
Because the Sloughi is a breed with a smooth coat, grooming is relatively simple. It includes brushing, bathing, trimming the

A natural and enjoyable form of exercise for Sloughis is practicing what they do best: coursing.

nails, cleaning the teeth and controlling ticks and fleas. In areas with strong changes in temperature between seasons, Sloughis grow an undercoat in winter, which they shed in spring or summer. During these transitions between seasons, the coat needs more care. Your goal is to make every grooming activity a pleasurable one. It is sensible to start by getting your puppy accustomed to it. Teaching these things to an adult dog makes it a much more challenging endeavor.

Routine brushing is good for your Sloughi's coat, and the dog grows to love the feel of being brushed and the one-on-one attention. You can use a natural bristle brush or a hound glove. Brushing the Sloughi's coat gets rid of dead hair and stimulates the coat's natural oils for a healthy look.

BATHING

Bathing is not something you need to do often with a Sloughi. Bathing removes some of the natural oils that work as a natural "raincoat" for your dog. It is best to bathe at the change of seasons, if the dog soils himself or before you go to a show. Do not use shampoos designed for human hair. Instead, choose from the variety of shampoos made specifically for dogs. In Sloughis, a protein

A good comb or rake is helpful in removing dead hair from the coat during times of shedding the undercoat.

lanolin shampoo will provide great results.

Brush your Sloughi before bathing to get rid of any dead hair. Provide a non-slip surface for your dog to stand on. Use a shower attachment to wet the coat thoroughly, all the while checking that the temperature is neither too hot nor too cold for the dog. In wetting the dog, start with the neck area, then proceed over the entire body.

Lather thoroughly with the shampoo all over the body, including the hard-to-reach places. Leave the head for last, as you do not want shampoo dripping in your dog's eyes or ears while you are concentrating on other parts of his body. Shampooing the head should be done very carefully, using your hands to prevent the flow of water mixed with shampoo to reach the eyes or the ear canals. Rinse thoroughly and remove the extra water by hand, then finally dry with a towel. Keep your Sloughi confined to a warm dry place until he is completely dry; never let a wet Sloughi outside in cold weather.

Nails

Trimming the nails is essential. Long nails cause the feet to spread and the toes to twist, and they can break and bleed or cause injuries to the toes themselves. A Sloughi with long nails can unintentionally hurt a human being or another dog if the dog scratches with his paw, or can cause damage if he tears in the fabric of your favorite sofa. Nails cut too short are not a good idea either, as the dog can slip when running at full speed. Dogs who live and run on hard surfaces typically have shorter nails than those who run only on grass, so it is a matter of checking regularly to find out when clipping is necessary. The correct length of a Sloughi's nails is just barely above the surface of the ground when the dog stands.

Your smooth-coated Sloughi does not require extensive grooming, but you will need to have basic equipment on hand.

There are two ways of trimming nails, cutting them or grinding them. Before you start any of these procedures, make sure you have identified the quick in each nail. The quick is the part of the toe inside the nail that is highly irrigated with blood and has nerve endings. The tip of the quick is what you want to avoid cutting because it will be painful to the dog. Cutting nails is done with a clipping tool that has a razor blade or a sharp metal blade. You simply cut the nails just below the end of the quick. The grinding tool uses a band of replaceable sanding paper. Grinding a dog's nails gives them a neater look. You can also clip and then grind, particularly if the nails are very long.

When a dog's nails are overly long, trim them stepwise, as the quick grows with the length of the nail. First trim to the quick, then wait a few days until the quick has receded somewhat. Then cut or grind again, and repeat until the nails are the correct length. When you trim, make sure your dog is comfortable and does not jerk his leg away as you are cutting. If you accidentally clip the tip of the quick, it will hurt, but it is not life-threatening. You should calm your dog, wait a little while and then resume cutting. Most of the time, the

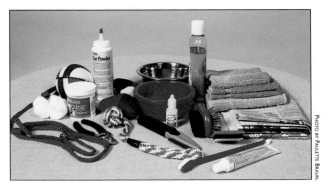

PHOTO BY PAULETTE BRAUN

blood clots fast. If it doesn't, you may want to use a clotting agent such as styptic powder (the kind used for shaving), for example.

EYE AND EAR CARE

During grooming sessions, pay extra attention to the condition of your dog's eyes. If the area around the eyes is soiled or if tear staining has occurred, there are various cleaning agents made especially to correct such conditions. Look at the dog's eyes to make sure no debris has entered; dogs who spend lots of time outdoors are especially prone to this.

The signs of an eye infection are obvious: mucus, redness, puffiness, scabs or other signs of irritation. If your dog's eyes become infected, the vet will likely prescribe an antibiotic ointment for treatment. If you notice signs of more serious problems, such as opacities in the eye, which usually indicate cataracts, consult the vet at once. Taking time to pay attention to your dog's eyes will alert you in the early stages of any problem so that you can get your dog treatment as soon as possible. You could save your dog's sight!

Routine checks are important for your dog's ears as well. A good time to check your dog's ears is during your grooming sessions, and of course the vet will check them during routine visits. If you see your dog shaking his ears often or scratching them repeatedly, those are signs that might indicate bacterial or mite infections, best treated by your vet.

A CLEAN SMILE

Another essential part of grooming is brushing your dog's teeth and checking his overall oral condition. Studies show that around 80% of dogs experience dental problems by two years of age, and the percentage is higher in older dogs. Therefore, it is highly likely that your dog will have trouble with his teeth and gums unless you are proactive with home dental care.

The most common dental problem in dogs is plaque build-up. If not treated, this causes gum disease, infection and resultant tooth loss. Bacteria from these infections can spread throughout the body, affecting the vital organs, possibly even causing death. Do you need much more convincing to start brushing your dog's teeth? If so, take a good whiff of your dog's breath and read on.

Fortunately, home dental care is rather easy and convenient for pet owners. Specially formulated canine

A hound glove removes dead hair and debris from the coat while massaging the dog and imparting a lovely sheen.

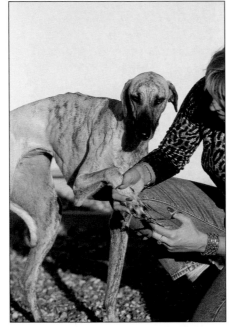

Use care in trimming the dog's nails. Your local pet shop will have suitable nail-clipping devices for canines.

toothpaste is easy to find. You should use one of these, not a product for humans. Some doggie pastes are even available in flavors appealing to dogs. If he likes the flavor, he will tolerate the process better, making things much easier for you. Doggie toothbrushes come in different sizes and are designed to fit the contours of a canine mouth. Rubber fingertip brushes fit right on one of your fingers and have rubber nodes to clean the teeth and massage the gums. This may be easier to handle, as it is akin to rubbing your dog's teeth with your finger.

As with other grooming tasks, accustom your pup to his dental care early on. Start gently, for a few minutes at a time, so that he gets used to the feel of the brush and to your handling his mouth. Offer praise and petting so that he looks at tooth-care time as a time when he gets extra love and attention. The routine should become second nature; at the very least, he should tolerate his teeth being brushed.

Aside from brushing, offer dental toys to your dog and feed crunchy biscuits, which help to minimize plaque. Rope toys have the added benefit of acting like floss as the dog chews. At your adult dog's yearly check-ups, the vet will likely perform a thorough tooth scraping as well as a complete check for any problems. Proper care of your dog's teeth will ensure that you will enjoy your dog's smile for many years to come. The next time your Sloughi goes to give you a hello kiss, you'll be glad you spent the time caring for his teeth.

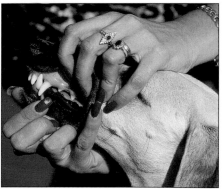

IDENTIFICATION FOR YOUR DOG

You love your dog and want to keep him safe. Of course you take every precaution to prevent his escaping from the yard or becoming lost or stolen. You have a sturdy high fence and you always keep your dog on lead when out and about in public places. However, if your dog is not properly identified you are overlooking a major aspect of his safety. We hope to never be in a situation where our dog is missing, but we should practice prevention in the unfortunate case that this happens; identification greatly increases the chances of your dog's being returned to you.

There are several ways to identify your dog. First, the traditional dog tag should be a staple in your dog's wardrobe, attached to his everyday collar. Tags can be made of sturdy plastic or various metals, and should include your contact information so that a person who finds the dog can get in touch with you right away to arrange his return. Many people today enjoy the wide range of decorative tags available, so have fun and create a tag to match your dog's personality. Of course, it is important that the tag stays on the collar, so have a secure "O" ring attachment; you also can explore the type of tag

Use utmost caution if using a cotton swab to clean the ears, as there is danger of injury if you probe into the ear canal or if the pup fidgets.

Care for your dog's teeth regularly. A weekly check on the teeth and gums will acclimate your Sloughi to the routine.

that slides right onto the collar.

In addition to the ID tag, which every dog should wear even if identified by another method, two other forms of identification have become popular: microchipping and tattooing. In microchipping, a tiny scannable chip is painlessly inserted under the dog's skin between the shoulder blades. The number is registered to you so that, if your lost dog turns up at a clinic or shelter, the chip can be scanned to retrieve your contact information.

The advantage of the microchip is that it is a permanent form of ID, but there are some factors to consider. Several different companies make microchips, and not all are compatible with the others' scanning devices. It's best to find a company with a universal microchip that can be read by scanners made by other companies as well. It won't do any good to have the dog chipped if the information cannot be retrieved. Also, not every humane society, shelter and clinic is equipped with a scanner, although more and more facilities are equipping themselves. In fact, many shelters microchip dogs that they adopt out to new homes.

In the US, there are five or six major microchip manufacturers as well as a few

databases. The American Kennel Club's Companion Animal Recovery unit works in conjunction with HomeAgain™ Companion Animal Retrieval System (Schering-Plough). In the UK, The Kennel Club is affiliated with the National Pet Register, operated by Wood Green Animal Shelters.

Humane societies and veterinary clinics offer microchipping, which is usually very affordable. Because the microchip is not visible to the eye, the dog must wear a tag that states that he is microchipped so that whoever picks him up will know to have him scanned. He of course also should have an ID tag with contact information in case his chip cannot be read.

Though less popular than microchipping, tattooing is another permanent method of ID for dogs. Most vets perform this service, and there are also clinics that perform dog tattooing. This is also an affordable procedure and one that will not cause much discomfort for the dog. It is best to put the tattoo in a visible area, such as the ear, to deter theft. It is sad to say that there are cases of dogs' being stolen and sold to research laboratories, but such laboratories will not accept tattooed dogs.

To ensure that the tattoo is

effective in aiding your dog's return to you, the tattoo number must be registered with a national organization. This way, when someone finds a tattooed dog, a phone call to the registry will quickly match the dog with his owner.

BOARDING

Today there are many options for dog owners who need someone to care for their dogs in certain circumstances. While many think of boarding their dogs as something to do when away on vacation, many others use the services of doggie "daycare" facilities, dropping their dogs off to spend the day while they are at work. Many of these facilities offer both long-term and daily care. Many go beyond just boarding and cater to all sorts of needs, with on-site grooming, veterinary care, training classes and even "web-cams" where owners can log onto the Internet and check out what their dogs are up to. Most dogs enjoy the activity and time spent with other dogs.

Before you need to use such a service, check out the ones in your area. Make visits to see the facilities, meet the staff, discuss fees and available services and see if this is a place where you think your dog will be happy. It is best to do your research in advance so that you're not stuck

at the last minute, forced to make a rushed decision without knowing if the kennel that you've chosen meets your standards. You also can check with your vet's office to see if they offer boarding for their clients or if they can recommend a good kennel in the area.

The kennel will need to see proof of your dog's health records and vaccinations so as not to spread illness from dog to dog. Your dog also will need proper identification. Owners usually experience some separation anxiety the first time they have to leave their dog in someone else's care, so it's reassuring to know that the kennel you choose is run by experienced, caring, true dog people.

A common identification technique is to have the dog tattooed with a number that then is registered with a national database. The ear is one of the most common locations, as the tattoo is easily visible there.

TRAINING YOUR

SLOUGHI

Begin training your Sloughi at an early age, as this results in the highest rate of success in developing well-mannered and well-adjusted adult dogs. Training an older dog— say, six months to six years of age— can produce almost equal results, provided that the owner accepts the dog's slower rate of learning capability and is willing to work patiently to help the dog succeed at developing to his fullest potential. Unfortunately, many owners of untrained adult dogs lack the patience factor, so they do not persist until their dogs are successful at learning particular behaviors.

Training a puppy aged 10 to 16 weeks (20 weeks at the most) is like working with a dry sponge in a pool of water. The pup soaks up whatever you show him and constantly looks for more things to do and learn. At this early age, his body is not yet producing hormones, and therein lies the reason for such a high rate of success. Without hormones, he is focused on his owners and not particularly interested in investigating other dogs, people, etc. You are his leader: his provider of food, water, shelter and security. He latches onto you and

wants to stay close. He will usually follow you from room to room, will not let you out of his sight when you are outdoors with him and will respond in like manner to the people and animals you encounter. If you greet a friend warmly, it encourages your Sloughi to warm up to that person. If, however, you are hesitant or anxious about the approach of a stranger, he will respond accordingly.

Once the puppy begins to produce hormones, his natural curiosity emerges and he begins to investigate the world around him. It is at this time when you may notice that the untrained dog begins to wander away from you and even ignore your commands to stay close. When this behavior becomes a problem, the owner has two choices: get rid of the dog or train him. It is strongly urged that you choose the latter option.

You can usually find obedience classes within a reasonable distance from your home, but you can also do a lot to train your dog yourself. Sometimes there are classes available, but the tuition is too costly. Whatever the circumstances, the solution to training your Sloughi without formal obedience classes lies within the pages of this book.

This chapter is devoted to helping you train your Sloughi at home. If the recommended procedures are followed faithfully, you may expect positive results that will prove rewarding to both you and your dog. Whether your new charge is a puppy or a mature adult, the methods of teaching and the techniques we use in training basic behaviors are the same. Positive training methods are the only course for a Sloughi, since no dog, regardless of breed and whether puppy or adult, likes harsh or inhumane methods, least of all the sensitive Sloughi. All creatures respond favorably to gentle motivational methods and sincere praise and encouragement.

HOUSE-TRAINING

Dogs are touch-oriented when it comes to house-training. In other words, they respond to the surface on which they are given approval to eliminate. The choice is yours (the dog's version is in parentheses): The lawn (including the neighbors' lawns)? A bare patch of earth under a tree (where people like to sit and relax in the summertime)? Concrete steps or patio (all sidewalks, garage and basement floors)? The curbside (watch out for cars)? A small area of crushed stone in a corner of the yard (mine!)? The latter is the best choice if you can manage it, because it will remain strictly for the dog's use and is easy to keep clean.

You can start out with paper-training indoors and switch over to an outdoor surface as the puppy matures and gains control over his need to eliminate. For the nay-sayers, don't worry—this won't mean that the dog will soil on every piece of newspaper lying around the house. You are training him to go outside, remember? Starting out by paper-training often is the only choice for a city dog.

WHEN YOUR PUPPY'S "GOT TO GO"
Your puppy's need to relieve himself is seemingly non-stop, but signs of improvement will be seen each week. From 8 to 10 weeks old, the puppy will have to be taken outside every time he wakes up, about 10–15 minutes after every

Attention is the key to all training, and with a sighthound you may have to be a bit more creative to get your pup's attention.

meal and after every period of play—all day long, from first thing in the morning until his bedtime! That's a total of ten or more trips per day to teach the puppy where it's okay to relieve himself. With that schedule in mind, you can see that house-training a young puppy is not a part-time job. It requires someone to be home all day.

If that seems overwhelming or impossible, do a little planning. For example, plan to pick up your puppy at the start of a vacation period. If you can't get home in the middle of the day, plan to hire a dog-sitter or ask a neighbor to come over to take the pup outside, feed him his lunch and then take him out again about ten or so minutes after he's eaten. Also make arrangements with that person or another to be your "emergency" contact if you have to stay late on the job. Remind yourself—repeatedly—that this hectic schedule improves as the puppy gets older. Be patient!

LEASH TRAINING

House-training and leash training go hand in hand, literally. When taking your puppy outside to do his business, lead him there on his leash. Unless an emergency potty run is called for, do not whisk the puppy in your arms and take him outside. If you have a fenced yard, you have the advantage of letting the puppy loose to go out, but it's better to put the dog on the leash and take him to his designated place in the yard until he is reliably house-trained. Taking the puppy for a walk is the best way to house-train a dog. The dog will associate the walk with his time to relieve himself and the exercise of walking stimulates the dog's bowels and bladder. Dogs that are not trained to relieve themselves on a walk may hold it until they get back home, which of course defeats half the purpose of the walk.

HOME WITHIN A HOME

Your puppy needs to be confined to one secure, puppy-proof area when no one is able to watch his every move. Generally, the kitchen is the place of choice because the floor is washable. Likewise, it's a busy family area that will accustom the pup to a variety of noises, everything from pots and pans to the telephone, blender and dishwasher. He will also be enchanted by the smell of your cooking (and will never be critical when you burn something). An

With a trained adult dog, the potty routine will be just that—routine. He will be used to his daily schedule and usual relief site.

exercise pen (also called an "ex-pen," a puppy version of a playpen) within the room of choice is an excellent means of confinement for a young pup. He can see out and has a certain amount of space in which to run about, but he is safe from dangerous things like electrical cords, heating units, trash baskets or open kitchen-supply cabinets. Place the pen in an area where the puppy will not get a blast of heat or air conditioning.

In the pen, you can put a few toys, his bed (which can be his crate if the dimensions of pen and crate are compatible) and a few layers of newspaper in one small corner, just in case. A water bowl can be hung at a convenient height on the side of the ex-pen so it won't become a splashing pool for an innovative puppy. His food dish can go on the floor, but not under the water bowl.

Crates are something that pet owners are at last getting used to for their dogs. Wild or domestic canines have always preferred to sleep in den-like safe spots, and that is exactly what the crate provides. How often have you seen adult dogs that choose to sleep under a table or chair even though they have full run of the house? It's the den connection that makes crate training work.

The crate can be solid (fiber-glass) with ventilation on the upper sides and a wire-grate door that locks securely, or it can be of open wire construction with a solid floor. Your puppy will go along with

CALM DOWN

Dogs will do anything for your attention. If you reward the dog when he is calm and attentive, you will develop a well-mannered dog. If, on the other hand, you greet your dog excitedly and encourage him to wrestle with you, the dog will greet you the same way and you will have a hyperactive dog on your hands.

whichever one you prefer. The open wire crate, however, should be covered at night to give the snug feeling of a den. A blanket or towel over the top will be fine.

The crate should be big enough for the adult dog to stand up and turn around in, even though he may spend much of his time curled up in the back part of it. There are movable barriers that fit inside dog crates to provide the right amount of space for small puppies that grow into large dogs. Never afford a

Your puppy looks up to his first teacher, his mom. When he becomes part of your family pack, you want him to look to you as his leader in the same way.

young puppy too much space, thinking that you're being kind and generous. He'll just sleep at one end of the crate and soil in the other end. While you should purchase only one crate, one that will accommodate your pup when grown, you will need to make use of the partitions so that the pup has a comfortable area without enough extra space to use as a toilet. A dog does not like to soil where he sleeps, so you are teaching him to "hold it" until it's time for a trip outside. You may want an extra crate to keep in the car for safe traveling.

In your "happy" voice, use the word "Crate" every time you put the pup in his den. If he's new to a crate, toss in a small biscuit for him to chase the first few times. At night, after he's been outside, he should sleep in his crate. The crate may be kept in his designated area at night or, if you want to be sure to hear those wake-up yips in the morning, put the crate in a corner of your bedroom. However, don't make any response whatsoever to whining or crying. If he's completely ignored, he'll settle down and get to sleep.

Good bedding for a young puppy is an old folded bath towel or an old blanket, something that is easily washable and disposable if necessary ("accidents" will happen!). Never put newspaper in the puppy's crate. Those old ideas of adding a clock to replace his mother's heartbeat, or a hot-water bottle to replace her warmth, are just that—old ideas. The clock could drive the puppy nuts, and the hot-water bottle could end up as a very soggy waterbed! An extremely good breeder would have introduced your puppy to the crate by letting two pups sleep together for a couple of nights, followed by several nights alone. How thankful you will be if you found that breeder!

Safe toys in the pup's crate or area will keep him occupied, but monitor their condition closely. Discard any toys that show signs of being chewed to bits. Squeaky parts, bits of stuffing or plastic or any other small pieces can cause intestinal blockage or possibly choking if swallowed.

CANINE DEVELOPMENT SCHEDULE

It is important to understand how and at what age a puppy develops into adulthood.
If you are a puppy owner, consult the following Canine Development Schedule to
determine the stage of development your puppy is currently experiencing.
This knowledge will help you as you work with the puppy in the weeks and months ahead.

PERIOD	AGE	CHARACTERISTICS
FIRST TO THIRD	BIRTH TO SEVEN WEEKS	Puppy needs food, sleep and warmth and responds to simple and gentle touching. Needs mother for security and disciplining. Needs littermates for learning and interacting with other dogs. Pup learns to function within a pack and learns pack order of dominance. Begin socializing pup with adults and children for short periods. Pup begins to become aware of his environment.
FOURTH	EIGHT TO TWELVE WEEKS	Brain is fully developed. Pup needs socializing with outside world. Remove from mother and littermates. Needs to change from canine pack to human pack. Human dominance necessary. Fear period occurs between 8 and 12 weeks. Avoid fright and pain.
FIFTH	THIRTEEN TO SIXTEEN WEEKS	Training and formal obedience should begin. Less association with other dogs, more with people, places, situations. Period will pass easily if you remember this is pup's change-to-adolescence time. Be firm and fair. Flight instinct prominent. Permissiveness and over-disciplining can do permanent damage. Praise for good behavior.
JUVENILE	FOUR TO EIGHT MONTHS	Another fear period about 7 to 8 months of age. It passes quickly, but be cautious of fright and pain. Sexual maturity reached. Dominant traits established. Dog should understand sit, down, come and stay by now.

NOTE: THESE ARE APPROXIMATE TIME FRAMES. ALLOW FOR INDIVIDUAL DIFFERENCES IN PUPPIES.

Although the Sloughi is not a breed that should spend too much time in a crate, the crate is still beneficial in many ways, and it is most useful when pups are introduced to crates early in life.

PROGRESSING WITH POTTY-TRAINING

After you've taken your puppy out and he has relieved himself in the area you've selected, he can have some free time with the family as long as there is someone responsible for watching him. That doesn't mean just someone in the same room who is watching TV or busy on the computer, but one person who is doing nothing other than keeping an eye on the pup, playing with him on the floor and helping him understand his position in the pack.

This first taste of freedom will let you begin to set the house rules. If you don't want the dog on the furniture, now is the time to prevent his first attempts to jump up on the couch. The word to use in this case is "Off," not "Down." "Down" is the word you will use to teach the down position, which is something entirely different.

Most corrections at this stage come in the form of simply distracting the puppy. Instead of telling him "No" for "Don't chew the carpet," distract the chomping puppy with a toy and he'll forget about the carpet.

As you are playing with the pup, do not forget to watch him closely and pay attention to his body language. Whenever you see him begin to circle or sniff, take the puppy outside to relieve himself. If you are paper-training, put him back in his confined area on the newspapers. In either case, praise him as he eliminates, while he actually is in the act of relieving himself. Three seconds after he has finished is too late! You'll be praising him for running toward you, or picking up a toy or whatever he may be doing at that moment, and that's not what you want to be praising him for. Timing is a vital tool in all dog training. Use it!

Remove soiled newspapers immediately and replace them with clean ones. You may want to take a small piece of soiled paper and place it in the middle of the new clean papers, as the scent will attract him to that spot when it's time to go again. That scent attraction is why it's so important to clean up any messes made in the house with a product specially made to eliminate the odor of dog urine and droppings. Regular household cleansers won't do the trick. Pet shops sell the best pet deodorizers. Invest in a large container; it won't go to waste.

Scent attraction eventually will lead your pup to his chosen spot outdoors; this is the basis of outdoor training. When you take your puppy outside to relieve himself, use a one-word command such as "Outside" or "Go-potty" (that's one word to the puppy!) as you pick him up and attach his leash. Then put him down in his area. If for any reason you can't carry him, snap the leash on quickly and lead him to his spot. Now comes the hard part—hard for you, that is. Just stand there until he urinates and defecates. Move him a

few feet in one direction or another if he's just sitting there, looking at you, but remember that this is neither playtime nor time for a walk. This is strictly a business trip! Then, as he circles and squats (remember your timing), give him a quiet "Good dog" as praise. If you start to jump for joy, ecstatic over his performance, he'll do one of two things: either he will stop mid-stream, as it were, or he'll do it again for you—in the house—and expect you to be just as delighted!

Give him five minutes or so and, if he doesn't go in that time, take him back indoors to his confined area and try again in another ten minutes, or immediately if you see him sniffing and circling. By careful observation, you'll soon work out a successful schedule.

Accidents, by the way, are just that—accidents. Clean them up quickly and thoroughly, without comment, after the puppy has been taken outside to finish his business and then put back in his area or

Clean living with any dog is based on teaching the dog that the outdoors is the proper place to go for toileting.

crate. If you witness an accident in progress, say "No!" in a stern voice and get the pup outdoors immediately. No punishment is needed. You and your puppy are just learning each other's language and sometimes it's easy to miss a puppy's message. Chalk it up to experience and vow to watch more closely from now on.

KEEPING THE PACK ORDERLY

Discipline is a form of training that brings order to life. For example, military discipline is what allows the soldiers in an army to work as one. Discipline is a form of teaching and, in dogs, is the basis of how the successful pack operates. Each member knows his place in the pack and all respect the leader, or Alpha dog. It is essential for your puppy that you establish this type of relationship, with you as the Alpha, or leader. It is a form of social coexistence that all canines recognize and accept. Discipline, therefore, is never to be confused with punishment. When you teach your puppy how you want him to behave, and he behaves properly and you praise him for it, you are disciplining him with a form of positive reinforcement.

For a dog, rewards come in the form of praise, a smile, a cheerful tone of voice, a few friendly pats or a rub of the ears. Rewards are also small food treats. Obviously, that does not mean bits of regular dog food. Rather, treats are very small bits of special things like cheese or pieces of soft dog treats. The idea is to reward the dog with something very small that he can taste and swallow, providing instant positive reinforcement. If he has to take time to chew the treat, by the time he is finished he will have forgotten what he did to earn it.

Your puppy should never be physically punished. The displeasure shown on your face and in your voice is sufficient to signal to the pup that he has done something wrong. He wants to please everyone higher up on the social ladder, especially his leader, so a scowl and

---

TIPS FOR TRAINING AND SAFETY

1. On or off leash, practice only in a fenced area.
2. Remove the training collar when the training session is over.
3. Don't try to separate fighting dogs.
4. "Come," "Leave it" and "Wait" are safety commands.
5. The dog belongs in a crate or behind a barrier when riding in the car.
6. Don't ignore the dog's first sign of aggression. Aggression only gets worse, so take it seriously.
7. Keep the faces of children and dogs separated.
8. Pay attention to what the dog is chewing.
9. Keep the vet's number near your phone.
10. "Okay" is a useful release command.

harsh voice will take care of the error. Growling out the word "Shame!" when the pup is caught in the act of doing something wrong is better than the repetitive "No." Some dogs hear "No" so often that they begin to think it's their name! By the way, do not use the dog's name when you're correcting him. His name is reserved to get his attention for something pleasant about to take place.

There are punishments that have nothing to do with you. For example, your dog may think that chasing cats is one reason for his existence. You can try to stop it as much as you like without success, because it's such fun for the dog. But one good hissing, spitting, swipe of a cat's claws across the dog's nose will put an end to the game forever. Only intervene when your dog's eyeball is seriously at risk. Cat scratches can cause permanent damage to an innocent but annoying puppy.

PUPPY KINDERGARTEN

COLLAR AND LEASH

Before you begin your puppy's education, he must be used to his collar and leash. Choose a collar for your puppy that is secure, but not heavy or bulky. He won't enjoy training if he's uncomfortable. A flat buckle collar is fine for everyday wear and for initial puppy training. For older dogs, there are several types of training collars such as the

Accustom your Sloughi pup to a lightweight lead and collar. He may resist at first, but soon he will not even notice that he's wearing it.

martingale, used often with sighthounds, which is a double loop that tightens slightly around the neck, or the head collar, which is similar to a horse's halter. Do not use a chain choke collar unless you have been specifically shown how to put it on and how to use it.

A lightweight 6-foot woven cotton or nylon training leash is preferred by most trainers because it is easy to fold up in your hand and comfortable to hold because there is a certain amount of give to it. There are lessons where the dog will start off six feet away from you at the end of the leash. The leash used to take the puppy outside to relieve himself is shorter because you don't want

The simplest way to focus your Sloughi's attention on you is with a treat, of course!

from the breeder, so you should be able to get his attention by saying his name—with a big smile and in an excited tone of voice. His response will be the puppy equivalent of "Here I am! What are we going to do?" Your immediate response (if you haven't guessed by now) is "Good dog." Rewarding him at the moment he pays attention to you teaches him the proper way to respond when he hears his name.

him to roam away from his area. The shorter leash will also be the one to use when you walk the puppy, and for the same reason.

If you've enrolled in a Puppy Kindergarten Training class, suggestions will be made as to the best collar and leash for your young puppy. These training classes are recommended because your puppy will be in a class with puppies in his age range (up to five months old) of all breeds and sizes. It's the perfect way for him to learn the right way (and the wrong way) to interact with other dogs as well as their people. You cannot teach your puppy how to interpret another dog's sign language. For a first-time puppy owner, these socialization classes are invaluable. For experienced dog owners, they are a real boon to further training.

EXERCISES FOR A BASIC CANINE EDUCATION

THE SIT EXERCISE

There are several ways to teach the puppy to sit. The first one is to catch him whenever he is about to sit and, as his backside nears the floor, say "Sit, good dog!" That's positive reinforcement and, if your timing is sharp, he will learn that what he's doing at that second is connected to your saying "Sit" and that you think he's clever for doing it.

Another method is to start with the puppy on his leash in front of you. Show him a treat in the palm of your right hand. Bring your hand up under his nose and, almost in slow motion, move your hand up and back so his nose goes up in the air and his head tilts back as he follows the treat in your hand. At that point, he will have to either sit or fall over, so as his back legs buckle under, say "Sit, good dog," and then give him the treat and lots of praise. You may have to begin

ATTENTION

You've been using the dog's name since the minute you collected him

with your hand lightly running up his chest, actually lifting his chin up until he sits. Some large (and usually older) dogs require gentle pressure on their hindquarters with the left hand, in which case the dog should be on your left side. Puppies generally do not appreciate this physical dominance.

After a few times, you should be able to show the dog a treat in the open palm of your hand, raise your hand waist-high as you say "Sit" and have him sit. In this way you have taught him two things at the same time. The verbal command and the motion of the hand are both signals for the sit. Your puppy is watching you almost more than he is listening to you, so what you do is just as important as what you say.

Don't save any of these drills only for training sessions. Use them as much as possible at odd times during a normal day. The dog should always sit before being given his food dish. He should sit to let you go through a doorway first, when the doorbell rings or when you stop to speak to someone on the street.

THE DOWN EXERCISE

Before beginning to teach the down command, you must consider how the dog feels about this exercise. To him, "down" is a submissive position. Being flat on the floor with you standing over him is not his idea of fun. It's up to you to let him know that, while it may not be fun, the reward of your approval is worth his effort.

Start with the puppy on your left side in a sit position. Hold the leash right above his collar in your left hand. Have an extra-special treat, such as a small piece of cooked chicken or hot dog, in your right hand. Place it at the end of the pup's nose and steadily move your hand down and forward along the ground. Hold the leash to prevent a sudden lunge for the food. As the puppy goes into the down position, say "Down" very gently.

The difficulty with this exercise is twofold: It's both the submissive

"SCHOOL" MODE

When is your puppy ready for a lesson? Maybe not always when you are. Attempting training with treats just before his mealtime is asking for disaster. Notice what times of day he performs best and make that Fido's school time.

aspect and the fact that most people say the word "Down" as if they were a drill sergeant in charge of recruits. So issue the command sweetly, give him the treat and have the pup maintain the down position for several seconds. If he tries to get up immediately, place your hands on his shoulders and press down gently, giving him a very quiet "Good dog." As you progress with this lesson, increase the "down time" until he will hold it until you say "Okay" (his cue for release). Practice this one in the house at various times throughout the day.

By increasing the length of time during which the dog must maintain the down position, you'll find many uses for it. For example, he can lie at your feet in the vet's office or anywhere else that both of you have to wait, when you are on the phone, while the family is eating and so forth. If you progress to training for competitive obedience, he'll already be all set for the exercise called the "long down."

THE STAY EXERCISE

To teach the sit/stay, have the dog sit on your left side. Hold the leash at waist level in your left hand and let the dog know that you have a treat in your closed right hand. Step forward on your right foot as you say "Stay." Immediately turn and stand directly in front of the dog, keeping your right hand up high so he'll keep his eye on the treat hand and maintain the sit position for a

count of five. Return to your original position and offer the reward.

Increase the length of the sit/stay each time until the dog can hold it for at least 30 seconds without moving. After about a week of success, move out on your right foot and take two steps before turning to face the dog. Give the "Stay" hand signal (left palm back toward the dog's head) as you leave. He gets the treat when you return and he holds the sit/stay. Increase the distance that you walk away from him before turning until you reach the length of your training leash. Don't rush it! Go back to the beginning if he moves before he should. No matter what the lesson, never be upset by having to back up for a few days. The repetition and practice are what will make your dog reliable in these commands. It won't do any good to move on to something more difficult if the command is not mastered at the easier levels. Above all, even if you do get frustrated, never let your puppy know. Always keep a positive, upbeat attitude during training, which will transmit to your dog for positive results.

The down/stay is taught in the same way once the dog is completely reliable and steady with the down command. Again, don't rush it. With the dog in the down position on your left side, step out on your right foot as you say "Stay." Return by walking around in back of the dog and into your original position. While you are training, it's okay to murmur something like "Hold on" to encourage him to stay put. When the dog will stay without moving when you are at a distance of 3 or 4 feet, begin to increase the length of time before you return. Be sure he holds the down on your return until you say "Okay." At that point, he gets his treat—just so he'll remember for next time that it's not over until it's over.

THE COME EXERCISE

No command is more important to the safety of your dog than "Come." It is what you should say every single time you see the puppy running toward you: "Binky, come! Good dog." During playtime, run a few feet away from the puppy, turn and tell him to come as he is already running to you. You can go so far as to teach your puppy two things at once if you squat down and hold out your arms. As the pup gets close to you and you're saying "Good dog," bring your right arm in about waist-high. Now he's also learning the hand signal, an excellent device should you be on the phone when you need to get him to come to you. You'll also both be one step ahead when you enter obedience classes.

Puppies, like children, have notoriously short attention spans, so don't overdo it with any of the training. Keep each lesson short. Break it up with a quick run around the yard or a ball toss, repeat the lesson and quit as soon as the pup gets it right.

That way, you will always end with a "Good dog."

When the puppy responds to your well-timed "Come," try it with the puppy on the training leash. This time, catch him off guard, while he's sniffing a leaf or watching a bird: "Binky, come!" You may have to pause for a split second after his name to be sure you have his attention. If the puppy shows any sign of confusion, give the leash a mild jerk and take a couple of steps backward. Do not repeat the command. In this case, as he reaches you, you should say "Good come!"

It's important to mention that an essential rule of training is that each command word is given just once. Anything more is nagging. You'll also notice that all commands are one word only. Even when they are actually two words, you say them as one.

The come command can be reinforced in many ways through play, such as engaging the dog in a game with one of his favorite toys.

Never call the dog to come to you—with or without his name—if you are angry or intend to correct him for some misbehavior. When correcting the pup, you go to him. Your dog must always connect "Come" with something pleasant and with your approval; then you can rely on his response. Life isn't

COME AND GET IT!

The come command is your dog's safety signal. Until he is 99% perfect in responding, don't use the come command if you cannot enforce it. Practice on leash with treats or squeakers, or whenever the dog is running to you. Never call him to come to you if he is to be corrected for a misdemeanor. Reward the dog with a treat and happy praise whenever he comes to you. While teaching the "come" is necessary, sighthound owners know that "off leash" means "on a mission" and that once the dog is off and running, he is likely to ignore your command.

perfect and neither are puppies. A time will come, often around 10 months of age, when he'll become "selectively deaf" or choose to "forget" his name. He may respond by wagging his tail (and even seeming to smile at you) with a look that says "Make me!" Laugh, throw his favorite toy and skip the lesson you had planned. Pups will be pups!

THE HEEL EXERCISE

The second most important command to teach, after the come, is the heel. When you are walking your growing puppy, you need to be in control. Besides, it looks terrible to be pulled and yanked down the street, and it's not much fun either! Your eight-to ten-week old puppy will probably follow you everywhere, but that's his natural instinct, not your control over the situation. However, any time he does follow you, you can say "Heel" and be ahead of the game, as he will learn to associate this command with the action of following you before you even begin teaching him to heel.

There is a very precise, almost military, procedure for teaching your dog to heel. As with other obedience training, begin with the dog on your left side. He will be in a very nice sit and you will have the training leash across your chest. Hold the loop and folded leash in your right hand. Pick up the slack leash above the dog in your left hand and hold it loosely at your side. Step out on your left foot as you say "Heel." If the puppy does not move, give a gentle tug or pat your left leg to get him started. If he surges ahead of you, stop and pull him back gently until he is at your side. Tell him to sit and begin again.

Walk a few steps and stop while the puppy is correctly beside you. Tell him to sit and give mild verbal praise. (More enthusiastic praise will encourage him to think the lesson is over.) Repeat the lesson, only increasing the number of steps you take as long as the dog is heeling nicely beside you. When you end the lesson, have him hold the sit, then give him the "Okay" to let him know that this is the end of the lesson. Praise him so that he knows he did a good job.

The cure for excessive pulling (a common problem) is to stop when the dog is no more than 2 or 3 feet ahead of you. Guide him back into position and begin again. With a really determined puller, try switching to a head collar. This will automatically turn the pup's head toward you so you can bring him back easily to the heel position. Give quiet, reassuring praise every time the leash goes slack and he's staying with you.

Staying and heeling can take a lot out of a dog, so provide playtime and free-running exercise when the lessons are over to shake off the stress. You don't want him to associate training with all work and no fun.

OBEDIENCE CLASSES

The advantages of an obedience class are that your dog will have to learn amid the distractions of other people and dogs and that your mistakes will be quickly corrected by the trainer. Teaching your dog along with a qualified instructor and other handlers who may have more dog experience than you is a further plus of the class environment. The instructor and other handlers can help you to find the most efficient way of teaching your dog a command or exercise. It's often easier to learn by other people's mistakes than your own. You will also learn all of the requirements for competitive obedience trials, in which you can earn titles and go on to advanced jumping and retrieving exercises, which are fun for many dogs. Obedience classes build the foundation needed for many other canine activities (in which we humans are allowed to participate, too!).

Teaching your large, strong and quick Sloughi to walk politely on lead is essential unless you want your dog to take *you* for a walk.

Sloughis watching the course in action. Each dog wears a blanket of either pink, blue or yellow.

Two Sloughis coursing the lure; a lure of white plastic is used in the US.

Two Sloughis being hand-slipped. In the US, this is done at the "Tally Ho" given by the huntmaster.

TRAINING FOR SPECIAL EVENTS

In the US, the Sloughi breed is integrated in all events designed for sighthounds, as well as straight racing and hunting, the latter two not permitted in Europe. The sighthound sporting events include racing, coursing and open field hunts. Racing and coursing events test the prey drive of sighthounds though the use of a "bunny" lure. These fake bunnies can be of various kinds, such as a piece of fur, a piece of white plastic or a piece of fur with a squawker. As the lure is propelled around the track, it stimulates the dogs' chasing instinct and the Sloughis just love it!

As in other sports, each of these venues involves both specialized training and conditioning, each association having its own rules to ensure this before the dog can be entered in an official event. Racing events are organized by various racing associations. They award the dogs various championship points or titles, depending on how well the dog does. They have nothing to do with the Greyhound racing industry. In Europe, most of the racing events are on oval of 380 to 480 meters long. In the US, the oval tracks are shorter, some 300 to 350 yards long. In racing, what counts is sheer speed, and the winner is the one who crosses the finish line first. Judges watch the dogs as they run to spot potential interference; they do not judge speed, but rather whether the dogs race "clean." In other words, they check to see whether the dogs interfere with their competitors or not. Inspection committees in each club organizing such events check for lame animals or bitches in season, which are removed from the competition. The titles and points awarded to the winners vary from country to country, as do the rules for disqualifications of interfering and/or aggressive dogs. In the US, Sloughis have an additional venue in the sprint or straight track racing on a course that is 200–250 yards long. On the oval tracks in Europe, Sloughis start from boxes; in the US, they can also be hand-slipped.

Coursing usually takes place on a large field. In the US, courses can be as long as up to 1200 yards. Each course varies from event to event at the discretion of each club; the designs of the courses include various combinations of turns and straight lines. The judges evaluate the dogs in coursing according to various criteria such as follow, agility, desire and speed. There also are rules about interference.

In most cases the lure is pulled in front of the dogs by a lure machine; in France sometimes the lure is pulled in front of the dogs by a rider on horseback. Some coursing events in Europe include jumping over obstacles such as bales of hay. In the US, the Sloughi can also be entered in open field hunts on hares. Again, the various associations have their own rules as to how

to evaluate each hunting hound.

The chasing instinct is only one of many aspects of the behavior of this versatile breed. Apart from these sighthound-specific performance events, Sloughis can be trained for other types of activities available to non-sighthound breeds as well. Sloughis participate in obedience, agility, tracking (they have a good sense of smell), herding and therapy work.

Just as a dog needs some amount of training to present himself properly in the show ring, to enable the judge to give him a fair assessment, all of the aforementioned activities require commitment and resources from the owner and trainer. Big wins in these events do not come out of the blue. Instead, they are the result of combined excellent breeding/genetics, proper raising, thorough socializing and dedication, knowledge and time in training. In addition, a trainer's good eye will help determine in which of these various activities a specific Sloughi is showing particular talent and potential.

In racing in the US, dogs usually start from boxes.

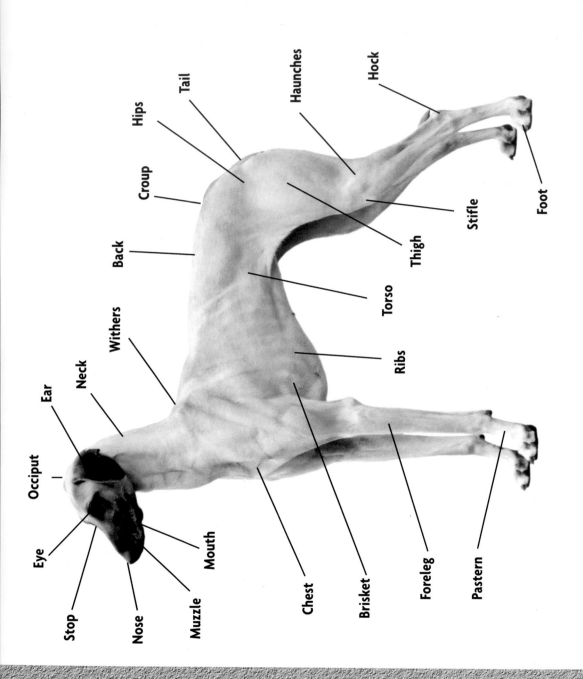

Occiput

Ear

Neck

Withers

Back

Croup

Hips

Tail

Haunches

Hock

Stifle

Foot

Thigh

Torso

Ribs

Eye

Stop

Nose

Muzzle

Mouth

Chest

Brisket

Foreleg

Pastern

PHYSICAL STRUCTURE OF THE SLOUGHI

HEALTHCARE OF YOUR

SLOUGHI

By Lowell Ackerman DVM, DACVD

HEALTHCARE FOR A LIFETIME
When you own a Sloughi, you become his healthcare advocate over his entire lifespan, as well as being the one to shoulder the financial burden of such care. Accordingly, it is worthwhile to focus on prevention rather than treatment, as you and your pet will both be happier.

Of course, the best place to have begun your program of preventive healthcare is with the initial purchase or adoption of your dog. There is no way of guaranteeing that your new furry friend is free of medical problems, but there are some things you can do to improve your odds. You certainly should have done adequate research into your breed of choice and have selected your puppy carefully. Health issues aside, a large number of pet abandonment and relinquishment cases arise from a mismatch between pet needs and owner expectations. This is entirely preventable with appropriate planning and finding a good breeder.

Regarding healthcare issues specifically, it is very difficult to make blanket statements about where to acquire a problem-free pet, but, again, a reputable breeder is your best bet. In an ideal situation, you have the opportunity to see both parents, get references from other owners of the breeder's pups and see genetic-testing documentation for several generations of the litter's ancestors. At the very least, you must thoroughly investigate the Sloughi and the problems inherent in that breed, as well as the genetic testing available to screen for those problems, such as PRA and hypothyroidism. Genetic testing offers some important benefits, but testing is only available for a few disorders in a relatively small number of breeds and is not available for some of the most common genetic diseases, such as hip dysplasia, cataracts, epilepsy, cardiomy-opathy, etc. This area of research is indeed exciting and increasingly important, and advances will continue to be made each year. In fact, recent research has shown that there is an equivalent

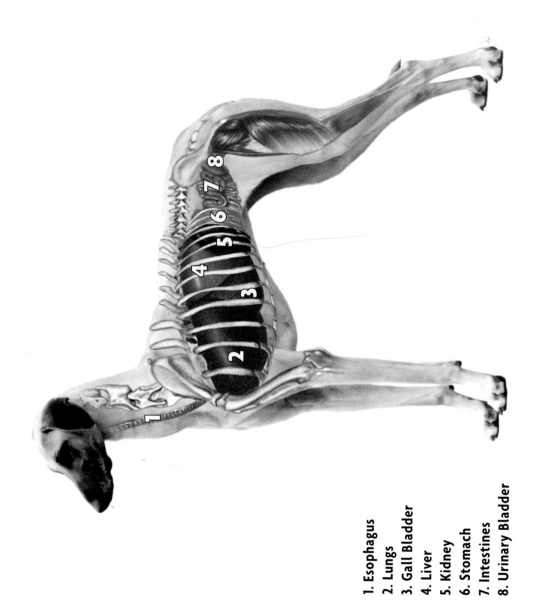

1. Esophagus
2. Lungs
3. Gall Bladder
4. Liver
5. Kidney
6. Stomach
7. Intestines
8. Urinary Bladder

INTERNAL ORGANS OF THE SLOUGHI

dog gene for 75% of known human genes, so research done in either species is likely to benefit the other.

We've also discussed that evaluating your chosen pup's behavioral nature and that of his immediate family members is an important part of the selection process that cannot be underestimated or overemphasized. It is sometimes difficult to evaluate temperament in puppies because certain behavioral tendencies, such as some forms of aggression, may not be immediately evident. More dogs are euthanized each year for behavioral reasons than for all medical conditions combined, so it is critical to take temperament issues seriously. Start with a well-balanced, friendly companion and put the time and effort into proper socialization, and you will both be rewarded with a lifelong valued relationship.

With a pup from healthy, sound stock, you become responsible for helping your veterinarian keep your pet healthy. Some crucial things happen before you even bring your puppy home. Parasite control typically begins at two weeks of age and vaccinations typically begin at six to eight weeks of age. A pre-pubertal evaluation is typically scheduled for about six months of age. At this time, a dental evaluation is done (since the adult teeth are now in), heartworm prevention is started, and neutering or spaying is usually done around this age.

It is critical to commence regular dental care at home if you have not already done so. It may not sound important, but most dogs have active periodontal disease by four years of age if they don't have their teeth cleaned regularly at home, in addition to at their veterinary exams. Dental problems lead to more than just bad "doggie breath"; gum disease can have very serious medical consequences. If you start brushing your dog's teeth and using antiseptic rinses from a young age, your dog will be accustomed to it and will not resist. The results will be healthy dentition, which your pet will need to enjoy a long, healthy life.

Most dogs are considered adults at a year of age, although some larger breeds still have some filling out to do up to about two or so years old. Each breed has different healthcare requirements, so work with your vet to determine what will be needed for your Sloughi and what your role should be. This doctor-client relationship is important, because as vaccination guidelines change there may not be an annual "vaccine visit" scheduled. You must make sure that you see your veterinarian at least annually, even if no vaccines are due, because this is the best opportu-

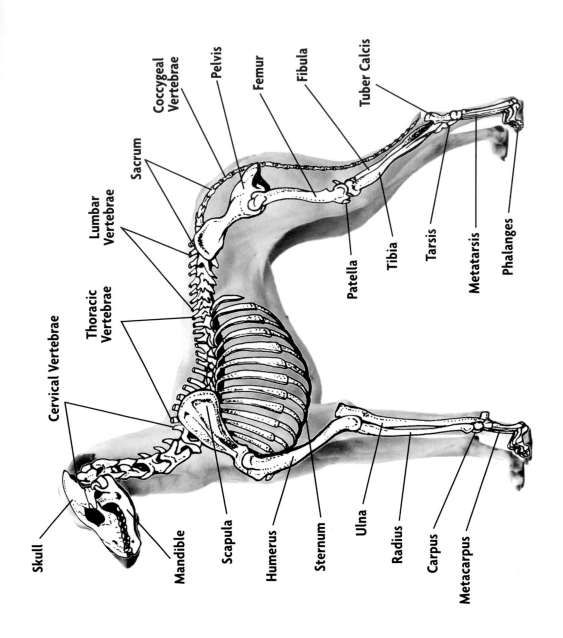

Coccygeal Vertebrae
Pelvis
Femur
Fibula
Tuber Calcis
Sacrum
Lumbar Vertebrae
Patella
Tibia
Tarsis
Metatarsis
Phalanges
Thoracic Vertebrae
Cervical Vertebrae
Skull
Mandible
Scapula
Humerus
Sternum
Ulna
Radius
Carpus
Metacarpus

SKELETAL STRUCTURE OF THE SLOUGHI

nity to coordinate healthcare activities and to make sure that no medical issues creep by unaddressed.

When your pet reaches three-quarters of his anticipated lifespan, he is considered a "senior" and likely requires some special care. In general, if you've been taking great care of your canine companion throughout his formative and adult years, the transition to senior status should be a smooth one. Age is not a disease, and as long as everything is functioning as it should, there is no reason why most of late adulthood should not be rewarding for both you and your pet. This is especially true if you have tended to the details, such as regular veterinary visits, proper dental care, excellent nutrition and management of bone and joint issues.

At this stage in your dog's life, your veterinarian may want to schedule visits twice yearly, instead of once, to run some laboratory screenings, electrocardiograms and the like, and to change the diet to something more digestible. Catching problems early is the best way to manage them effectively. Treating the early stages of heart disease is so much easier than trying to intervene when there is more significant damage to the heart muscle. Similarly, managing the beginning of kidney problems is fairly

routine if there is no significant kidney damage. Other problems, like cognitive dysfunction (similar to senility and Alzheimer's disease), cancer, diabetes and arthritis, are more common in older dogs, but all can be treated to help the dog live as many happy, comfortable years as possible. Just as in people, medical management is more effective (and less expensive) when you catch things early.

SELECTING A VETERINARIAN

There is probably no more important decision that you will make regarding your pet's health-care than the selection of his doctor. Your pet's veterinarian will be a pediatrician, family-practice physician and gerontologist, depending on the dog's life stage, and will be the individual who makes recommendations regarding issues such as when specialists need to be consulted, when diagnostic testing and/or

GO AND TELL YOUR VET
Because Sloughis are very lean, they are, like other sighthounds, very sensitive to anesthesia. After surgery, they are prone to hypothermia. It is important that your vet is aware of this and that he uses anesthetics designed for sighthounds if surgery is required on your Sloughi. He must also monitor your Sloughi's temperature after surgery.

therapeutic intervention is needed and when you will need to seek outside emergency and critical-care services. Your vet will act as your advocate and liaison throughout these processes.

Everyone has his own idea about what to look for in a vet, an individual who will play a big role in his dog's (and, of course, his own) life for many years to come. For some, it is the compassionate caregiver with whom they hope to develop a professional relationship to span the lifetime of their dogs and even their future pets. For others, they are seeking a clinician with keen diagnostic and therapeutic insight who can deliver state-of-the-art healthcare. Still others need a veterinary facility that is open evenings and weekends, or is in close proximity or provides mobile veterinary services, to accommodate their schedules; these people may not much mind that their dogs might see different veterinarians on each visit. Just as we have different reasons for selecting our own healthcare professionals (e.g., covered by insurance plan, expert in field, convenient location, etc.), we should not expect that there is a one-size-fits-all recommendation for selecting a veterinarian and veterinary practice. The best advice is to be honest in your assessment of what you expect from a veterinary practice and to conscientiously research the options in your area. You will quickly appreciate that not all veterinary practices are the same and you will be happiest with one that truly meets your needs and the needs of your Sloughi.

There is another point to be considered in the selection of veterinary services. Not that long ago, a single veterinarian would attempt to manage all medical and surgical issues as they arose. That was often problematic, because veterinarians are trained in many breed, species and diseases, and it

TAKING YOUR DOG'S TEMPERATURE

It is important to know how to take your dog's temperature at times when you think he may be ill. It's not the most enjoyable task, but can be done without too much difficulty. It's easier with a helper, preferably someone with whom the dog is friendly, so that one of you can hold the dog while the other inserts the thermometer.

Before inserting the thermometer, coat the end with petroleum jelly. Insert the thermometer slowly and gently into the dog's rectum about one inch. Wait for the reading, about two minutes. Be sure to remove the thermometer carefully and clean it thoroughly after each use.

A dog's normal body temperature is between 100.5 and 102.5 °F. Immediate veterinary attention is required if the dog's temperature is below 99 or above 104 °F.

was just impossible for general veterinary practitioners to be experts in every animal, every field and every ailment. However, just as in the human healthcare fields, specialization has allowed general practitioners to concentrate on primary healthcare delivery, especially wellness and the prevention of infectious diseases, and to utilize a network of specialists to assist in the management of conditions that require specific expertise and experience. Thus there are now many types of veterinary specialists, including dermatologists, cardiologists, ophthalmologists, surgeons, internists, oncologists, neurologists, behaviorists, criticalists and others to help primary-care veterinarians deal with complicated medical challenges. In most cases, specialists see cases referred by primary-care veterinarians, make diagnoses and set up management plans. From there, the animals' ongoing care is returned to their primary-care veterinarians. This important team approach to your pet's medical-care needs has provided opportunities for advanced care and an unparalleled level of quality to be delivered.

With all of the opportunities for your pet to receive high-quality veterinary medical care, there is another topic that needs to be addressed at the same time—cost. It's been said that you

Caring for a Sloughi means being attentive to his special needs as a naturally lean dog. It also means watching out for dangers that can be encountered outdoors, as the breed will need plenty of time for outdoor exercise.

can have excellent healthcare or inexpensive healthcare, but never both; this is as true in veterinary medicine as it is in human medicine. While veterinary costs are a fraction of what the same services cost in the human healthcare arena, it is still difficult to deal with unanticipated medical costs, especially since they can easily creep into hundreds or even thousands of dollars if specialists or emergency services become involved. However, there are ways of managing these risks. The easiest is to buy pet health insurance and realize that its foremost purpose is not to cover routine healthcare visits but rather to serve as an umbrella for those rainy days when your pet needs medical care and you don't want to worry about whether or not you can afford that care.

Pet insurance policies are very cost-effective (and very inexpensive by human health-insurance standards), but make sure that you buy the policy long before you intend to use it (preferably starting in puppyhood, because coverage will exclude pre-existing conditions) and that you are actually buying an indemnity insurance plan from an insurance company that is regulated by your state or province. Many insurance policy look-alikes are actually discount clubs that are only redeemable at specific locations and for specific services. An indemnity plan covers your pet at almost all veterinary, specialty and emergency practices and is an excellent way to manage your pet's ongoing healthcare needs.

VACCINATIONS AND INFECTIOUS DISEASES

There has never been an easier time to prevent a variety of infectious diseases in your dog, but these advances come with a price—choice. Now, while it may seem that choice is a good thing (and it is), it has never been more

DISEASE REFERENCE CHART

	WHAT IS IT?	WHAT CAUSES IT?	SYMPTOMS
Leptospirosis	Severe disease that affects the internal organs; can be spread to people.	A bacterium, which is often carried by rodents, that enters through mucous membranes and spreads quickly throughout the body.	Range from fever, vomiting and loss of appetite in less severe cases to shock, irreversible kidney damage and possibly death in most severe cases.
Rabies	Potentially deadly virus that infects warm-blooded mammals.	Bite from a carrier of the virus, mainly wild animals.	1st stage: dog exhibits change in behavior, fear. 2nd stage: dog's behavior becomes more aggressive. 3rd stage: loss of coordination, trouble with bodily functions.
Parvovirus	Highly contagious virus, potentially deadly.	Ingestion of the virus, which is usually spread through the feces of infected dogs.	Most common: severe diarrhea. Also vomiting, fatigue, lack of appetite.
Canine cough	Contagious respiratory infection.	Combination of types of bacteria and virus. Most common: *Bordetella bronchiseptica* bacteria and parainfluenza virus.	Chronic cough.
Distemper	Disease primarily affecting respiratory and nervous system.	Virus that is related to the human measles virus.	Mild symptoms such as fever, lack of appetite and mucus secretion progress to evidence of brain damage, "hard pad."
Hepatitis	Virus primarily affecting the liver.	Canine adenovirus type I (CAV-1). Enters system when dog breathes in particles.	Lesser symptoms include listlessness, diarrhea, vomiting. More severe symptoms include "blue-eye" (clumps of virus in eye).
Coronavirus	Virus resulting in digestive problems.	Virus is spread through infected dog's feces.	Stomach upset evidenced by lack of appetite, vomiting, diarrhea.

SAMPLE VACCINATION SCHEDULE

6–8 weeks of age	Parvovirus, Distemper, Adenovirus-2 (Hepatitis)
9–11 weeks of age	Parvovirus, Distemper, Adenovirus-2 (Hepatitis)
12–14 weeks of age	Parvovirus, Distemper, Adenovirus-2 (Hepatitis)
16-20 weeks of age	Rabies
1 year of age	Parvovirus, Distemper, Adenovirus-2 (Hepatitis), Rabies

Revaccination is performed every one to three years, depending on the product, the method of administration and the patient's risk. Initial adult inoculation (for dogs at least 16 weeks of age in which a puppy series was not done or could not be confirmed) is two vaccinations, done three to four weeks apart, with revaccination according to the same criteria mentioned. Other vaccines are given as decided between owner and veterinarian.

difficult for the pet owner (or the veterinarian) to make an informed decision about the best way to protect pets through vaccination. With the Sloughi, it is further complicated by the breed's tendency to be sensitive to anesthesia and other injections, something you must make sure that your vet knows from the outset.

Years ago, it was just accepted that puppies got a starter series of vaccinations and then annual "boosters" throughout their lives to keep them protected. As more and more vaccines became available, consumers wanted the convenience of having all of that protection in a single injection. The result was "multivalent" vaccines that crammed a lot of protection into a single syringe. The manufacturers' recommendations were to give the vaccines annually, and this was a simple enough protocol to follow. However, as veterinary medicine has become more sophisticated and we have started looking more at healthcare quandaries rather than convenience, it became necessary to reevaluate the situation and deal with some tough questions. It is important to realize that whether or not to use a particular vaccine depends on the risk of contracting the disease against which it protects, the severity of the disease if it is contracted, the duration of immunity provided by the vaccine, the safety of the product and the needs of the individual animal. In a very general sense, rabies, distemper, hepatitis and parvovirus are considered core vaccine needs, while parainfluenza, canine cough, Leptospirosis, coronavirus and borreliosis (Lyme disease) are considered non-core needs and best reserved for animals that demonstrate reasonable risk of contracting the diseases.

NEUTERING/SPAYING

Sterilization procedures (neutering for males/spaying for females) are meant to accomplish several purposes. While the underlying premise is to address the risk of pet overpopulation, there are also some medical and behavioral benefits to the surgeries as well. For females, spaying prior to the first estrus (heat cycle) leads to a marked reduction in the risk of mammary cancer.

When it's time for a trip to the vet, you'll need a dog-friendly mode of transportation. Safety gates are made to partition the rear section of a vehicle to create an area of safe confinement during travel.

There are also no manifestations of "heat" to attract male dogs and no bleeding in the house. For males, there is prevention of testicular cancer and a reduction in the risk of prostate problems. In both sexes, there may be some limited reduction in aggressive behaviors toward other dogs, and some diminishing of urine marking, roaming and mounting.

While neutering and spaying do indeed prevent animals from contributing to pet overpopulation, even no-cost and low-cost neutering options have not eliminated the problem. Perhaps one of the main reasons for this is that individuals who intentionally breed their dogs and those who allow their animals to run at large are the main causes of unwanted offspring. Also, animals in shelters are often there because they were abandoned or relinquished, not because they came from unplanned matings. Neutering/spaying is important, but it should be considered in the context of the real causes of animals' ending up in shelters and eventually being euthanized.

One of the important considerations regarding neutering is that it is a surgical procedure. This sometimes gets lost in discussions of low-cost procedures and commoditization of the process. In females, spaying is specifically referred to as an ovariohysterectomy. In this procedure, a midline incision is made in the abdomen and the entire uterus and both ovaries are surgically removed. While this is a major invasive surgical procedure, it usually has few complications, because it is typically performed on young healthy animals. However, it is a major surgery, as any woman who has had a hysterectomy will attest.

In males, neutering has traditionally referred to castration, which involves the surgical removal of both testicles. While still a significant piece of surgery, there is not the abdominal exposure that is required in the female surgery. In addition, there is now a chemical sterilization option, in which a solution is injected into each testicle, leading to atrophy of the sperm-producing cells. This can typically be done under sedation rather than full anesthesia. This is a relatively new approach, and there are no long-term clinical studies yet available.

Neutering/spaying is typically done around six months of age at most veterinary hospitals, although techniques have been pioneered to perform the procedures in animals as young as eight weeks of age. In general, the surgeries on the very young animals are done for the specific reason of sterilizing them before they go to their new homes. This is done in some shelter hospitals for assurance that the animals will definitely not produce any pups. Otherwise, these organi-zations need to rely on owners to comply with their wishes to have the animals "altered" at a later date, something that does not always happen.

There are some exciting immunocontraceptive "vaccines" currently under development, and there may be a time when contraception in pets will not require surgical procedures. We anxiously await these developments.

SKIN PROBLEMS IN SLOUGHIS
Vets are consulted by dog owners for skin problems more than for any other group of diseases or maladies. Dogs' skin is almost as sensitive as human skin and both can suffer from almost the same ailments (though acne in most breeds is rare). For this reason, veterinary dermatology has developed into a specialty practiced by many vets.

Since many skin problems have visual symptoms that are almost identical, it requires the skill of an experienced veterinary dermatologist to identify and cure many of the more severe skin disorders. Pet shops sell many treatments for skin problems, but most of the treatments are directed at symptoms and not the underlying problem(s). If your dog is suffering from a skin disorder, you should seek professional assistance as quickly as possible. As with other diseases, the earlier a problem is identified and treated, the more likely is a complete cure.

S. E. M. by Dr. Dennis Kunkel, University of Hawaii.

A scanning electron micrograph of a dog flea, *Ctenocephalides canis,* on dog hair.

EXTERNAL PARASITES

FLEAS

Fleas have been around for millions of years and, while we have better tools now for controlling them than at any time in the past, there still is little chance that they will end up on an endangered species list. Actually, they are very well adapted to living on our pets, and they continue to adapt as we make advances.

The female flea can consume 15 times her weight in blood during active reproduction and can lay as many as 40 eggs a day. These eggs are very resistant to the effects of insecticides. They hatch into larvae, which then mature and spin cocoons. The immature fleas reside in this pupal stage until the time is right for feeding. This pupal stage is also very resistant to the effects of insecticides, and pupae can last in the environment without feeding for many months. Newly emergent fleas are attracted to animals by the warmth of the animals' bodies, movement and exhaled carbon dioxide. However, when they first emerge from their cocoons, they orient towards light; thus when an animal passes between a flea and the light source, casting a shadow, the flea pounces and starts to feed. If the animal turns out to be a dog or cat, the reproductive cycle continues. If the flea lands on another type of animal, including a person, the flea will bite but will then look for a more appropriate host. An emerging adult flea can survive without feeding for up to 12 months but, once it tastes blood, it can survive off its host for only three to four days.

It was once thought that fleas spend most of their lives in the environment, but we now know that fleas won't willingly jump off a dog unless leaping to another dog or when physically removed by brushing, bathing or other manipulation. Flea eggs, on the other hand, are shiny and smooth, and they roll off the animal and into the environment. The eggs, larvae and pupae then exist in the environment, but once the adult finds a susceptible animal, it's home sweet home until the flea is convinced to seek refuge elsewhere.

Since adult fleas live on the animal and immature forms survive in the environment, a successful treatment plan must address all stages of the flea life cycle. There are now several safe and effective flea-control products that can be applied on a monthly

> ### FLEA PREVENTION FOR YOUR DOG
> - Discuss with your veterinarian the safest product to protect your dog, likely in the form of a monthly tablet or a liquid preparation placed on the back of the dog's neck
> - For dogs suffering from flea-bite dermatitis, a shampoo or topical insecticide treatment is required.
> - Your lawn and property should be sprayed with an insecticide designed to kill fleas and ticks that lurk outdoors.
> - Using a flea comb, check the dog's coat regularly for any signs of parasites.
> - Practice good housekeeping: vacuum floors, carpets and furniture regularly, especially in the areas that the dog frequents, and wash the dog's bedding weekly.
> - Follow up house-cleaning with carpet shampoos and sprays to rid the house of fleas at all stages of development. Insect growth regulators are the safest option.

basis. These include fipronil, imidacloprid, selamectin and permethrin (found in several formulations). Most of these products have significant flea-killing rates within 24 hours. However, none of them will control the immature forms in the environment. To accomplish this, there are a variety of insect growth regulators that can be

THE FLEA'S LIFE CYCLE

What came first, the flea or the egg? This age-old mystery is more difficult to comprehend than the actual cycle of the flea. Fleas usually live only about four months. A female can lay 2,000 eggs in her lifetime.

Egg

After ten days of rolling around your carpet or under your furniture, the eggs hatch into larvae, which feed on various and sundry debris. In days or months, depending on the climate, the larvae spin a cocoon and develop into the pupal or nymph stage, which quickly develop into fleas.

Larva

Pupa

These immature fleas must locate a host within 10 to 14 days or they will die. Only about 1% of the flea population exist as adult fleas, while the other 99% exist as eggs, larvae or pupae.

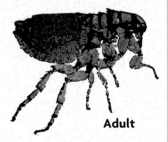

Adult

KILL FLEAS THE NATURAL WAY

If you choose not to go the route of conventional medication, there are some natural ways to ward off fleas:

• Dust your dog with a natural flea powder, composed of such herbal goodies as rosemary, wormwood, pennyroyal, citronella, rue, tobacco powder and eucalyptus.

• Apply diatomaceous earth, the fossilized remains of single-cell algae, to your carpets, furniture and pet's bedding. Even though it's not good for dogs, it's even worse for fleas, which will dry up swiftly and die.

• Brush your dog frequently, give him adequate exercise and let him fast occasionally. All of these activities strengthen the dog's system and make him more resistant to disease and parasites.

• Bathe your dog with a capful of pennyroyal or eucalyptus oil.

• Feed a natural diet, free of additives and preservatives. Add some fresh garlic and brewer's yeast to the dog's morning portion, as these items have flea-repelling properties.

sprayed into the environment (e.g., pyriproxyfen, methoprene, fenoxycarb) as well as insect development inhibitors such as lufenuron that can be administered. These compounds have no effect on adult fleas, but they stop immature forms from developing into adults. In years gone by, we relied heavily on toxic insecticides (such as organophosphates, organochlorines and carbamates) to manage the flea problem, but today's options are not only much safer to use on our pets but also safer for the environment.

TICKS

Ticks are members of the spider class (arachnids) and are blood-sucking parasites capable of transmitting a variety of diseases, including Lyme disease, ehrlichiosis, babesiosis and Rocky Mountain spotted fever. It's easy to see ticks on your own skin, but it is more of a challenge when your furry companion is affected. Whenever you happen to be planning a stroll in a tick-infested area (especially forests, grassy or wooded areas or parks) be prepared to do a thorough inspection of your dog afterward to search for ticks. Ticks can be tricky, so make sure you spend time looking in the ears, between the toes and everywhere else where a tick might hide. Ticks need to be attached for 24–72 hours before they transmit most of the diseases that they carry, so you do have a window of opportunity for some preventive intervention.

A TICKING BOMB

There is nothing good about a tick's harpooning his nose into your dog's skin. Among the diseases caused by ticks are Rocky Mountain spotted fever, canine ehrlichiosis, canine babesiosis, canine hepatozoonosis and Lyme disease. If a dog is allergic to the saliva of a female wood tick, he can develop tick paralysis.

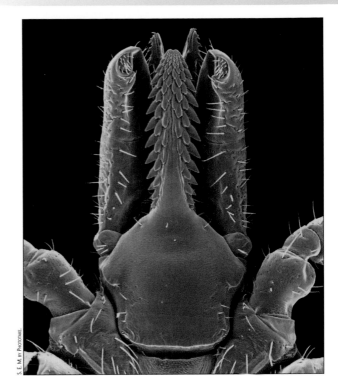

S. E. M. BY PHOTOTAKE.

A scanning electron micrograph of the head of a female deer tick, *Ixodes dammini*, a parasitic tick that carries Lyme disease.

Female ticks live to eat and breed. They can lay between 4,000 and 5,000 eggs and they die soon after. Males, on the other hand, live only to mate with the females and continue the process as long as they are able. Most ticks live on multiple hosts before parasitizing dogs. The immature forms typically reside on grass and shrubs, waiting for suscep-tible animals to walk by. The larvae and nymph stages typically feed on wildlife.

If only a few ticks are present on a dog, they can be plucked out, but it is important to remove the entire head and mouthparts,

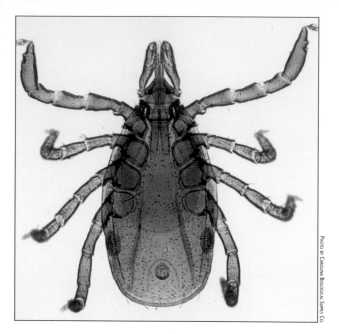

**Deer tick,
Ixodes dammini.**

PHOTO BY CAROLINA BIOLOGICAL SUPPLY CO.

which may be deeply embedded in the skin. This is best accomplished with forceps designed especially for this purpose; fingers can be used but should be protected with rubber gloves, plastic wrap or at least a paper towel. The tick should be grasped as closely as possible to the animal's skin and should be pulled upward with steady, even pressure. Do not squeeze, crush or puncture the body of the tick or you risk exposure to any disease carried by that tick. Once the ticks have been removed, the sites of attachment should be disinfected. Your hands should then be washed with soap and water to further minimize risk of contagion. The tick should be disposed of in a container of alcohol or household bleach.

Some of the newer flea products, specifically those with fipronil, selamectin and permethrin, have effect against some, but not all, species of tick. Flea collars containing appropriate insecticides (e.g., propoxur, chlorfenvinphos) can aid in tick control. In most areas, such collars should be placed on animals in March, at the beginning of the tick season, and changed regularly. Leaving the collar on when the insecticide level is waning invites the development of resistance. Amitraz collars are also good for tick control, and the active ingredient does not interfere with other flea-control products. The ingredient helps prevent the attachment of ticks to the skin and will cause those ticks already on the skin to detach themselves.

TICK CONTROL
Removal of underbrush and leaf litter and the thinning of trees in areas where tick control is desired are recommended. These actions remove the cover and food sources for small animals that serve as hosts for ticks. With continued mowing of grasses in these areas, the probability of ticks' surviving is further reduced. A variety of insecticide ingredients (e.g., resmethrin, carbaryl, permethrin, chlorpyrifos, dioxathion and allethrin) are registered for tick control around the home.

MITES

Mites are tiny arachnid parasites that parasitize the skin of dogs. Skin diseases caused by mites are referred to as "mange," and there are many different forms seen in dogs. These forms are very different from one another, each one warranting an individual description.

Sarcoptic mange, or scabies, is one of the itchiest conditions that affects dogs. The microscopic *Sarcoptes* mites burrow into the superficial layers of the skin and can drive dogs crazy with itchiness. They are also communicable to people, although they can't complete their reproductive cycle on people. In addition to being tiny, the mites also are often difficult to find when trying to make a diagnosis. Skin scrapings from multiple areas are examined microscopically but, even then, sometimes the mites cannot be found.

Fortunately, scabies is relatively easy to treat, and there are a variety of products that will successfully kill the mites. Since the mites can't live in the environment for very long without feeding, a complete cure is usually possible within four to eight weeks.

Cheyletiellosis is caused by a relatively large mite, which sometimes can be seen even without a microscope. Often referred to as "walking dandruff," this also causes itching, but not usually as profound as with scabies.

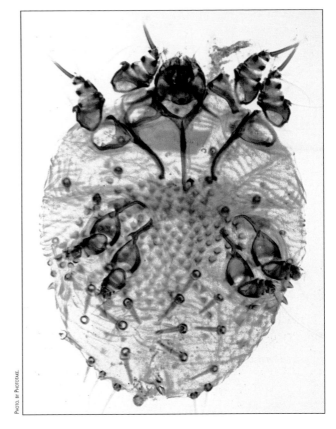

PHOTO. BY PHOTOTAKE.

Sarcoptes scabiei, commonly known as the "itch mite."

While *Cheyletiella* mites can survive somewhat longer in the environment than scabies mites, they too are relatively easy to treat, being responsive not only to the medications used to treat scabies but also often to flea-control products.

Otodectes cynotis is the canine ear mite and is one of the more common causes of mange, especially in young dogs in shelters or pet stores. That's because the mites are typically present in large numbers and are quickly spread to

Micrograph of a dog louse, *Heterodoxus spiniger*. Female lice attach their eggs to the hairs of the dog. As the eggs hatch, the larval lice bite and feed on the blood. Lice can also feed on dead skin and hair. This feeding activity can cause hair loss and skin problems.

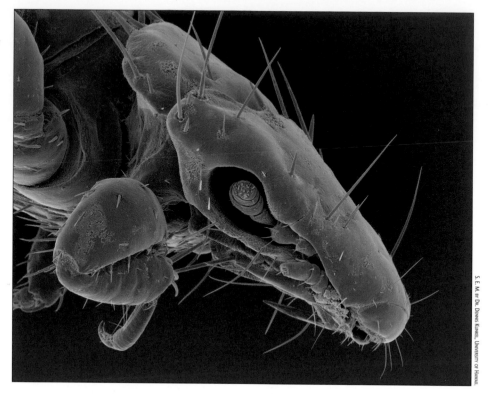

S. E. M. by Dr. Dennis Kunkel, University of Hawaii.

nearby animals. The mites rarely do much harm, but can be difficult to eradicate if the treatment regimen is not comprehensive. While many try to treat the condition with ear drops only, this is the most common cause of treatment failure. Ear drops cause the mites to simply move out of the ears and as far away as possible (usually to the base of the tail) until the insecticide levels in the ears drop to an acceptable level—then it's back to business as usual! The successful treatment of ear mites requires treating all animals in the household with a systemic insecticide, such as selamectin, or a combination of miticidal ear drops combined with whole-body flea-control preparations.

Demodicosis, sometimes referred to as red mange, can be one of the most difficult forms of mange to treat. Part of the problem has to do with the fact that the mites live in the hair follicles and are relatively well shielded from topical and systemic products. The main issue, however, is that demodectic mange typically results only when there is some underlying process interfering with the dog's immune system.

Since *Demodex* mites are normal residents of the skin of

mammals, including humans, there is usually a mite population explosion only when the immune system fails to keep the number of mites in check. In young animals, the immuno deficit may be transient or it may reflect an actual inherited immune problem. In older animals, demodicosis is usually seen only when there is another disease hampering the immune system, such as diabetes, cancer, thyroid problems or the use of immune-suppressing drugs. Accordingly, treatment involves not only trying to kill the mange mites but also discerning what is interfering with immune function and correcting it if possible.

Chiggers represent several different species of mite that don't parasitize dogs specifically, but do latch on to passersby and can cause irritation. The problem is most prevalent in wooded areas in the late summer and fall. Treatment is not difficult, as the mites do not complete their life cycle on dogs and are susceptible to a variety of insecticides.

MOSQUITOES

Mosquitoes have long been known to transmit a variety of diseases to people, as well as just being biting pests during warm weather. They also pose a real risk to pets. Not only do they carry deadly heartworms but

recently there also has been much concern over their involvement with West Nile virus. While we can avoid heartworm with the use of preventive medications, there are no such preventives for West Nile virus. The only method of prevention in endemic areas is active mosquito control. Fortunately, most dogs that have been exposed to the virus only developed flu-like symptoms and, to date, there have not been the large number of reported deaths in canines as seen in some other species.

Illustration of *Demodex folliculoram.*

MOSQUITO REPELLENT

Low concentrations of DEET (less than 10%), found in many human mosquito repellents, have been safely used in dogs but, in these concentrations, probably give only about two hours of protection. DEET may be safe in these small concentrations, but since it is not licensed for use on dogs, there is no research proving its safety for dogs. Products containing permethrin give the longest-lasting protection, perhaps two to four weeks. As DEET is not licensed for use on dogs, and both DEET and permethrin can be quite toxic to cats, appropriate care should be exercised. Other products, such as those containing oil of citronella, also have some mosquito-repellent activity, but typically have a relatively short duration of action.

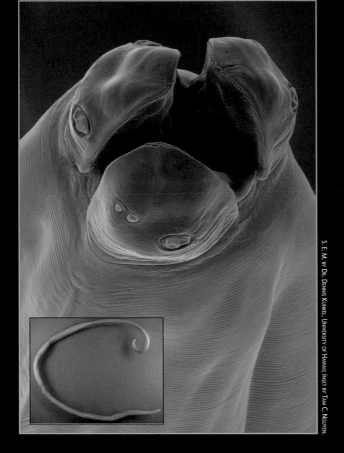

S. E. M. BY DR. DENNIS KUNKEL, UNIVERSITY OF HAWAII. INSET BY TAM C. NGUYEN.

ASCARID DANGERS

The most commonly encountered worms in dogs are roundworms known as ascarids. *Toxascaris leonine* and *Toxocara canis* are the two species that infect dogs. Subsisting in the dog's stomach and intestines, adult roundworms can grow to 7 inches in length and adult females can lay in excess of 200,000 eggs in a single day.

In humans, visceral larval migrans affects people who have ingested eggs of *Toxocara canis*, which frequently contaminates children's sandboxes, beaches and park grounds. The roundworms reside in the human's stomach and intestines, as they would in a dog's, but do not mature. Instead, they find their way to the liver, lungs and skin, or even to the heart or kidneys in severe cases. Deworming puppies is critical in preventing the infection in humans, and young children should never handle nursing pups who have not been dewormed.

The ascarid roundworm *Toxocara canis*, showing the mouth with three lips. INSET: Photomicrograph of the roundworm *Ascaris lumbricoides*.

INTERNAL PARASITES: WORMS

ASCARIDS

Ascarids are intestinal roundworms that rarely cause severe disease in dogs. Nonetheless, they are of major public health significance because they can be transferred to people. Sadly, it is children who are most commonly affected by the parasite, probably from inadvertently ingesting ascarid-contaminated soil. In fact, many yards and children's sandboxes contain appreciable numbers of ascarid eggs. So, while ascarids don't bite dogs or latch onto their intestines to suck blood, they do cause some nasty medical conditions in children and are best eradicated from our Sloughi friends. Because pups can start passing ascarid eggs by three weeks of age, most parasite-control programs begin at two weeks of age and are repeated every two weeks until pups are eight weeks old. It is important to

HOOKED ON ANCYLOSTOMA

Adult dogs can become infected by the bloodsucking nematodes we commonly call hookworms via ingesting larvae from the ground or via the larvae penetrating the dog's skin. It is not uncommon for infected dogs to show no symptoms of hookworm infestation. Sometimes symptoms occur within ten days of exposure. These symptoms can include bloody diarrhea, anemia, loss of weight and general weakness. Dogs pass the hookworm eggs in their stools, which serves as the vet's method of identifying the infestation. The hookworm larvae can encyst themselves in the dog's tissues and be released when the dog is experiencing stress.

Caused by an *Ancylostoma* species whose common host is the dog, cutaneous larval migrans affects humans, causing itching and lumps and streaks beneath the surface of the skin.

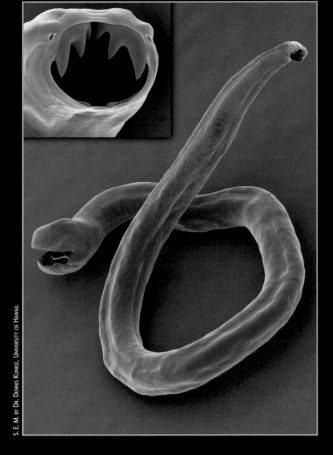

S. E. M. BY DR. DENNIS KUNKEL, UNIVERSITY OF HAWAII.

realize that bitches can pass ascarids to their pups even if they test negative prior to whelping. Accordingly, bitches are best treated at the same time as the pups.

HOOKWORMS

Unlike ascarids, hookworms do latch onto a dog's intestinal tract and can cause significant loss of blood and protein. Similar to ascarids, hookworms can be transmitted to humans, where they cause a condition known as cutaneous larval migrans. Dogs can become infected either by consuming the infective larvae or by the larvae's penetrating the skin directly. People most often get infected when they are lying on the ground (such as on a beach) and the larvae penetrate the skin. Yes, the larvae can penetrate through a beach blanket. Hookworms are typically susceptible to the same medications used to treat ascarids.

The hookworm *Ancylostoma caninum* infests the colon of dogs. INSET: Note the row of hooks at the posterior end, used to anchor the worm to the intestinal wall.

WHIPWORMS

Whipworms latch onto the lower aspects of the dog's colon and can cause cramping and diarrhea. Eggs do not start to appear in the dog's feces until about three months after the dog was infected. This worm has a peculiar life cycle, which makes it more difficult to control than ascarids or hookworms. The good thing is that whipworms rarely are transferred to people.

Some of the medications used to treat ascarids and hookworms are also effective against whipworms, but, in general, a separate treatment protocol is needed. Since most of the medications are effective against the adults but not the eggs or larvae, treatment is typically repeated in three weeks, and then often in three

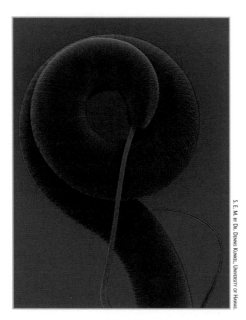

Adult whipworm, *Trichuris* sp., an intestinal parasite.

S. E. M. BY DR. DENNIS KUNKEL, UNIVERSITY OF HAWAII

> ## WORM CONTROL GUIDELINES
> - Practice sanitary habits with your dog and home.
> - Clean up after your dog and don't let him sniff or eat other dogs' droppings.
> - Control insects and fleas in the dog's environment. Fleas, lice, cockroaches, beetles, mice and rats can act as hosts for various worms.
> - Prevent dogs from eating uncooked meat, raw poultry and dead animals.
> - Keep dogs and children from playing in sand and soil.
> - Kennel dogs on cement or gravel; avoid dirt runs.
> - Administer heartworm preventatives regularly.
> - Have your vet examine your dog's stools at your annual visits.
> - Select a boarding kennel carefully so as to avoid contamination from other dogs or an unsanitary environment.
> - Prevent dogs from roaming. Obey local leash laws.

months as well. Unfortunately, since dogs don't develop resistance to whipworms, it is difficult to prevent them from getting reinfected if they visit soil contaminated with whipworm eggs.

TAPEWORMS

There are many different species of tapeworm that affect dogs, but *Dipylidium caninum* is probably the most common and is spread by fleas. Flea larvae feed on organic debris and tapeworm eggs in the environment and, when a dog chews at himself and manages to ingest fleas, he might get a dose of tapeworm at the same time. The tapeworm then develops further in the intestine of the dog.

The tapeworm itself, which latches onto the intestinal wall, is composed of numerous segments. When the segments break off into the intestine (as proglottids), they may accumulate around the rectum, like grains of rice. While this tapeworm is disgusting in its behavior, it is not directly communicable to humans (although humans can also get infected by swallowing fleas).

A much more dangerous flatworm is *Echinococcus multilocularis*, which is typically found in foxes, coyotes and wolves. The eggs are passed in the feces and infect rodents, and, when dogs eat the rodents, the dogs can be infected by thousands of adult tapeworms. While the parasites don't cause many problems in dogs, this is considered the most lethal worm infection that people can get. Take appropriate precautions if you live in an area in which these tapeworms are found. Do not use mulch that may contain feces of dogs, cats or wildlife, and discourage your pets from hunting

wildlife. Treat these tapeworm infections aggressively in pets, because if humans get infected, approximately half die.

HEARTWORMS

Heartworm disease is caused by the parasite *Dirofilaria immitis* and is seen in dogs around the world. A member of the roundworm group, it is spread between dogs by the bite of an infected mosquito. The mosquito injects infective larvae into the dog's skin with its bite, and these larvae develop under the skin for a period of time before making their way to the heart. There they develop into adults, which grow and create blockages of the heart, lungs and major blood vessels there. They also start producing offspring (microfilariae)

A dog tapeworm proglottid (body segment).

The dog tapeworm *Taenia pisiformis*.

S. E. M. BY DR. DENNIS KUNKEL, UNIVERSITY OF HAWAII.

A Look at Internal Parasites

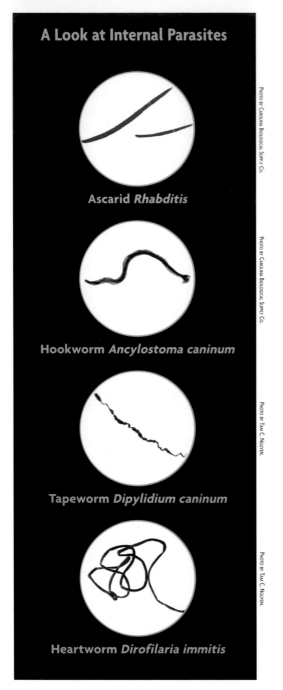

Ascarid *Rhabditis*

Hookworm *Ancylostoma caninum*

Tapeworm *Dipylidium caninum*

Heartworm *Dirofilaria immitis*

and these microfilariae circulate in the bloodstream, waiting to hitch a ride when the next mosquito bites. Once in the mosquito, the microfilariae develop into infective larvae and the entire process is repeated.

When dogs get infected with heartworm, over time they tend to develop symptoms associated with heart disease, such as coughing, exercise intolerance and potentially many other manifestations. Diagnosis is confirmed by either seeing the microfilariae themselves in blood samples or using immunologic tests (antigen testing) to identify the presence of adult heartworms. Since antigen tests measure the presence of adult heartworms and microfilarial tests measure offspring produced by adults, neither are positive until six to seven months after the initial infection. However, the beginning of damage can occur by fifth-stage larvae as early as three months after infection. Thus it is possible for dogs to be harboring problem-causing larvae for up to three months before either type of test would identify an infection.

The good news is that there are great protocols available for preventing heartworm in dogs. Testing is critical in the process, and it is important to understand the benefits as well as the limitations of such testing. All dogs six months of age or older that have not been on continuous heart-worm-preventive medication

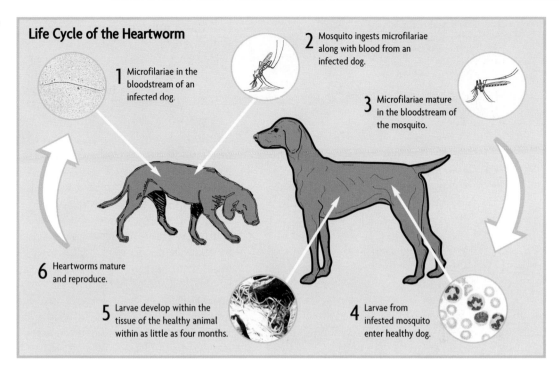

Life Cycle of the Heartworm

1 Microfilariae in the bloodstream of an infected dog.

2 Mosquito ingests microfilariae along with blood from an infected dog.

3 Microfilariae mature in the bloodstream of the mosquito.

4 Larvae from infested mosquito enter healthy dog.

5 Larvae develop within the tissue of the healthy animal within as little as four months.

6 Heartworms mature and reproduce.

should be screened with microfilarial or antigen tests. For dogs receiving preventive medication, periodic antigen testing helps assess the effectiveness of the preventives. The American Heartworm Society guidelines suggest that annual retesting may not be necessary when owners have absolutely provided continuous heartworm prevention. Retesting on a two- to three-year interval may be sufficient in these cases. However, your veterinarian will likely have specific guidelines under which heartworm preventives will be prescribed, and many prefer to err on the side of safety and retest annually.

It is indeed fortunate that heartworm is relatively easy to prevent, because treatments can be as life-threatening as the disease itself. Treatment requires a two-step process that kills the adult heartworms first and then the microfilariae. Prevention is obviously preferable; this involves a once-monthly oral or topical treatment. The most common oral preventives include ivermectin (not suitable for some breeds), moxidectin and milbemycin oxime; the once-a-month topical drug selamectin provides heartworm protection in addition to flea, tick and other parasite controls.

SHOWING YOUR

SLOUGHI

When you purchase your Sloughi, you will make it clear to the breeder whether you want one just as a lovable companion and pet, or if you hope to be buying a Sloughi with show prospects. No reputable breeder will sell you a young puppy and tell you that it is definitely of show quality, for so much can go wrong during the early months of a puppy's development. If you plan to show, what you will hopefully have acquired is a puppy with "show potential."

To the novice, exhibiting a Sloughi in the show ring may look easy, but it takes a lot of hard work and devotion to do top winning at a national specialty or an all-breed show.

The first concept that the novice exhibitor learns when watching a dog show is that each dog first competes against members of its own breed. Once the judge has selected the best member of each breed (Best of Breed), provided that the show is judged on a Group system, that chosen dog will compete with other dogs in its group. Finally, the dogs chosen first in each group will compete for Best in Show.

The second concept that you must understand is that the dogs are not actually compared against one another. The judge compares each dog against the breed standard, the written description of the ideal specimen that is approved by the hosting kennel club, such as the United Kennel Club (UKC), the Fédération Cynologique Internationale (FCI) or The Kennel Club (England). While some early breed standards were indeed based on specific dogs that were famous or popular, many dedicated enthusiasts say that a perfect specimen, as described in the standard, has never walked into a show ring, has never been bred and, to the woe of dog breeders around the globe, does not exist. Breeders attempt to get as close to this ideal as possible with every litter, but theoretically the "perfect" dog is so elusive that it is impossible. (And if the "perfect" dog were born, breeders and judges would never agree that it was indeed "perfect.")

If you are interested in exploring the world of dog showing, your best bet is to join your local breed club or a national club like

A Sloughi being presented at the Amsterdam International Championship Show, 2001.

FOR MORE INFORMATION....

For reliable up-to-date information about registration, dog shows and other canine competitions, contact one of the national registries by mail or via the Internet.

United Kennel Club
100 E. Kilgore Road, Kalamazoo, MI 49002
www.ukcdogs.com

American Kennel Club
5580 Centerview Dr., Raleigh, NC 27606-3390
www.akc.org

Canadian Kennel Club
89 Skyway Ave., Suite 100, Etobicoke, Ontario
M9W 6R4 Canada
www.ckc.ca

The Kennel Club
1-5 Clarges St., Piccadilly, London W1Y 8AB, UK
www.the-kennel-club.org.uk

Fédération Cynologique Internationale
14, rue Leopold II, B-6530 Thuin, Belgium
www.fci.be

the Sloughi Fanciers Association of America or the Sloughi Club in the UK. These clubs often host both regional and national specialties, shows only for Sloughis, which can include conformation as well as obedience and agility trials, lure coursing and racing events. Even if you have no intention of competing with your Sloughi, a specialty is like a festival for lovers of the breed who congregate to share their favorite topic: the Sloughi! Clubs also send out newsletters, and some organize training days and seminars in order that people may learn more about their chosen breed.

If your Sloughi is six months of age or older and registered with the UKC, The Kennel Club or FCI, you can enter him in a dog show where the breed is offered classes. Provided that your Sloughi does not have a disqualifying fault, he can compete. Only unaltered dogs can be entered in a dog show, so if you have spayed or neutered your Sloughi, your dog cannot compete in conformation shows. The reason for this is simple. Dog shows are the main forum to prove which representatives in a breed are worthy of being bred. Only dogs that have achieved championships—the dog world's "seal of approval" for quality in pure-bred dogs—should be bred. Altered dogs, however, can participate in certain other competitive events aside from conformation.

Before you actually step into the ring, you would be well advised to sit back and observe the judge's ring procedure. If it is your first time in the ring, stand back and study how the exhibitor in front of you is performing. The judge asks each handler to stand or "stack" the dog, hopefully showing the dog off to his best advantage. The judge will observe the dog from a distance and from different angles, and approach the dog to check his teeth, overall structure, alertness and muscle tone, as well as consider how well the dog "conforms" to the standard. Most importantly, the judge will have the exhibitor move the dog around the ring in

OPPORTUNITIES FOR JUNIORS

For budding dog handlers, as young as 2 years old and through 18 years old, the UKC's Total Junior program is an excellent training ground for the next generation of dog professionals. Owning and caring for a dog are wonderful methods of teaching children responsibility, and the Total Junior program builds upon that foundation. Juniors learn by grooming, training and handling their dogs, and the quality of the junior handler's presentation of the dog (and of himself) is evaluated by a licensed judge. More than just conformation showing, this program puts the emphasis on "total," with divisions for juniors offered in showmanship, agility, obedience and weight-pulling classes to encourage all-around participation and achievement in the canine sport. Aside from the competitive aspect, the importance of proper treatment of the dogs as well as good sportsmanship is stressed to the juniors.

Competition for juniors is divided into four age categories: Pee-Wee (ages 2 to under 4 years); Sub-Junior (ages 4 to under 8 years); Junior (ages 8 to under 13 years); and Senior (ages 13 to under 19 years). Showmanship classes for the Junior and Senior age groups are further divided into Novice and Open. Juniors can compete with any UKC-registered dog that is at least six months of age.

In addition to awards and points given out on show days, juniors can be eligible for other special awards. These include the Total Junior award, recognizing achievement in two or more areas of the sport; the Top Ten competition, a national competition among the top ten juniors in each of the four areas of competition; the Junior Service award, recognizing a junior's involvement in promoting responsible breeding, training and ownership of dogs; and the Junior Showmanship award, a peer-selected honor.

Regardless of the area of competition, dog and handler must work as a team, follow the judge's directions and display poise, confidence and consideration for other competitors. Those licensed to judge junior competition have a wonderful opportunity to teach and mold the future of the dog sport. Judges are encouraged to officiate in a manner that will help young people to continue to learn, to improve their handling skills and to increase their knowledge of show procedure and regulations.

some pattern that he should specify. Finally, the judge will give the dog one last look before moving on to the next exhibitor.

If you are not in the top four in your class at your first show, do not be discouraged. Be patient and consistent, and you may eventually find yourself in a winning line-up. Remember that the winners were once in your shoes and have devoted many hours and much money to earn the placement. If you find that your dog is losing every time and never getting a nod, it may be time to consider a different dog sport or to just enjoy your Sloughi as a pet. Parent clubs offer other events, such as lure coursing, agility, tracking, obedience, racing, instinct tests and more, which may be of interest to the owner of a well-trained Sloughi.

OBEDIENCE TRIALS

Obedience trials in the US trace back to the early 1930s when organized obedience training was developed to demonstrate how well dog and owner could work together. The pioneer of obedience trials is Mrs. Helen Whitehouse Walker, a Standard Poodle fancier,

The author poses with her Best-of-Breed winning dog at the SFAA's first national specialty in Woodstock, July 1998.

The judge is getting a full view of the outline of the dog as the handler adjusts the dog to the proper posture.

who designed a series of exercises after the Associated Sheep, Police, Army Dog Society of Great Britain. Since the days of Mrs. Walker, obedience trials have grown by leaps and bounds, and today there are thousands of trials held in the US alone every year, with more than 100,000 dogs competing. Any registered dog can enter an obedience trial, regardless of conformational disqualifications or neutering.

AGILITY TRIALS

Having had its origins in the UK back in 1977, the sport of agility was first promoted in the US by the United States Dog Agility Association, Inc. (USDAA), which

obstacle course that includes jumps as well as tires, the dog walk, weave poles, pipe tunnels, collapsed tunnels, etc. While working his way through the course, the dog must keep one eye and ear on the handler and the rest of his body on the course. The handler gives verbal and hand signals to guide the dog through the course.

Agility is great fun for dog and owner, with many rewards for everyone involved. Interested owners should join a training club that has obstacles and experienced agility handlers who can introduce you and your dog to the "ropes" (and tires, tunnels, etc.).

TRACKING
Any dog is capable of tracking, using his nose to follow a trail. Tracking tests are exciting and competitive ways to test your Sloughi's ability to search and rescue. The first tracking tests, back in 1937, took place as part of an obedience trial. In the beginning level of tracking, the owner follows the dog through a field on a long lead. To earn the title, the dog must follow a track laid by a human 30 to 120 minutes prior. The track is about 500 yards long with up to 5 directional changes. More advanced titles require that the dog follow a track that is 3 to 5 hours old over a course up to 1,000 yards long with up to 7 directional changes.

was established in 1986 and spawned numerous member clubs around the country. Three titles are available through the USDAA: Agility Dog (AD), Advanced Agility Dog (AAD) and Master Agility Dog (MAD). Dogs must be 18 months or older to be eligible for participation in USDAA events.

Agility is designed so that the handler demonstrates how well the dog can work at his side. The handler directs his dog over an

Balsam Shi' Rayàn, intently observing the events on the coursing field while awaiting her turn.

Sloughis in the
race in full swing.

Taking the turn in
oval racing.

In the US, all racing dogs are muzzled and four different blanket colors are used. They are numbered: red, 1; blue, 2; white, 3; green, 4. Here are four dogs, ready to race as the handler holds their muzzles.

A top athlete, in double suspension gallop typical of sighthounds, is Fahel Shi'Rayân, number-one all-time all-breeds in sprint racing in the US.

LURE COURSING

Lure-coursing events are open to all members of the sighthound family, including such breeds as the Scottish Deerhound, Greyhound, Whippet, Irish Wolfhound and, of course, the Sloughi. Chasing fleet-footed quarry is the born-for function of the Sloughi, and lure-coursing trials challenge and test the breed's natural instincts. All dogs must be one year of age to compete in these events. For more information on these trials, contact your breed club for their rules and regulations and a schedule of events in your area.

Sighthounds can participate in events sponsored by the American Sighthound Field Association (ASFA), an organization devoted to the pursuit of lure coursing. The ASFA was founded in 1972 as a means of keeping open field coursing dogs fit in the off-season. It has grown into the largest lure-coursing association in the world. Dogs must be of an accepted sighthound breed in order to be eligible for participation. Each dog must pass a certification run in which he shows that he can chase the lure with another dog without interfering.

Got it! In US sprint racing, the lure is made of fur with a squeaker hidden inside. The lure squawks as it bounces on the ground ahead of the dogs. The white plastic is mainly for the lure operator to see the location of the lure, but is also helpful in training dogs to follow the plastic lure used in coursing.

The course is laid out using pulleys and a motor to drive the string around the pulleys. Normally white plastic bags are used as lures, although real fur strips may also be attached. Dogs run in trios, each handled by their own slipper. The dogs are scored on their endurance, follow, speed, agility and enthusiasm. Dogs earn their Field Champion titles by earning two first places, or one first- and two second-place finishes, as well as accumulating 100 points. They can then go on to earn the title, Lure Courser of Merit, by winning four first places and accumulating 300 additional points.

Coursing is an all-day event, held in all weather conditions. It is great fun for the whole family, but on a rainy, cold day, it's best to leave the kids at home!

RACING

The Large Gazehound Racing Association (LGRA) and the National Oval Track Racing Association (NOTRA) are organizations that sponsor and regulate non-commercial dog races in the US. Races are usually either 200-yard sprints (LGRA) or semi- or complete ovals (NOTRA). The LGRA organizes sprint racing for other breeds than Whippets, who have their own sprint racing associations. The NOTRA organizes oval racing for Whippets and all the other breeds of sighthound it recognizes. In both LGRA and NOTRA races, the dogs generally run out of starting boxes, meaning that racing dogs must be trained to the box. Local racing clubs offer training programs that can assist novice owners and dogs.

Dogs compete in a draw of four each and are ranked according to their previous racing record. The lure in LGRA events consists of both real fur and a predator call. In NOTRA events, the lure is white plastic and often a fur strip. There are three programs and the dogs are rotated through the draw according to their finish in each preceding program. Dogs earn the Gazehound Racing Champion (GRC) or the Oval Racing Champion (ORC) title when they accumulate 12 championship points. Dogs can earn the most difficult titles of Supreme Oval Racing Champion (SORC) and Superior Gazehound Racing Champion (SGRC) by accumulating 30 National points.

Both LGRA and NOTRA races are owner-participation sports in which each owner plays some role: catcher, walker, line judge or foul judge. If you plan to race your dog, plan to work all day during a race day! There is little time for anything else, but the reward of seeing four dogs pour over the finish line shoulder to shoulder is more than enough.

INDEX

Activities 117, 148
Adult
—diet 90
—health 121
—training 100
Afghan Hound 13, **17**, 21
Aggression 89, 108, 128
Agility 117, 148
Aging 123
Algeria 9-11, 15-19
Allen, Captain, J. P. T. 41
Allergies 57
Alpha role 108
American Heartworm
  Society 143
American Kennel Club 39,
  146
American Rare Breed
  Association 41
American Sighthound Field
  Association 38, 154
American Sloughi
  Association 38
American Veterinary
  Medical Association 86
Amherst, Lady Florence 21,
  42, 47
Ancylostoma caninum **139**,
  142
Anesthesia sensitivity 53,
  86, 123
Antifreeze 85
Artificial insemination 30,
  36
Ascarid **138**, 139
Ascaris lumbricoides **138**
Attention 109-110, 113
Azawakh 13, 15, 19, **45**
—compared to Sloughi **44**
Babisia 10
Basenji **14**, 15
Bathing 93
Bedding 80, 88, 104
Bedouin 12, 15, 18-19, 48
Berbers 11, 13, 15, 19, 48
Best in Show 144
Best of Breed 144
Blindness 54
Bloat 91
Body language 106
Body temperature 124
Bones 81
Bordetella bronchiseptica
  126
Boredom 52
Borreliosis 128
Boulechfar, Gudrun 37
Bowls 78
Branding of legs 18
Breed club 144
—events 147
Breed standard 58, 144
Breeder 73, 144
—selection 72, 74, 119

Breeding practices 16, 18
Brooke, Mr. H. C. 41
Brushing 93
California 39
Canada 39
Canadian Kennel Club 146
Cancer 57, 128
Canine cough 126, 128
Canine development
  schedule 105
Car travel 108
Carthage 11
Chase instinct 47, 116-117
Chew toys 80, 103-104
Chewing 80, 108
Cheyletiella mite **135**
Chiggers 137
Children 50, 87, 89, 108
Chocolate 91
Cioce, Carole 38
Clarke, Vicki 39
Club du Sloughi 23
Club du Sloughi d'Alger 10
Club du Sloughi Marocain
  10, 15
Coat 19, 21, 49
Coat maintenance 93
Coget, Captain 9
Cognitive dysfunction 123
Cold weather 52
Collar **82-83**, 108-109
Colors 16-17, 49
Come 108, 113-114
Commands 110-115
Commitment of ownership
  74-75
Competitive activities 116
Cook-Schmidt, Gisela 38
Core vaccines 128
Cornevin, Charles 9, 22
Coronavirus 126, 128
Correction 109
Countries of origin 11, 15-17,
  21
Coursing 32, 116-117
Crate 50, 78, 87-88, 103
—pads 80
—training 101-108
Crying 88, 104
Ctenocephalides canis **130**
Curiosity 49
Dangers in the home 84-85
Daumas, Général 9, 17-19, 21
De Caprona, Dominique 41
De la Horde d'Or 23
De Lavallart, Mme. Simeon
  22, 28
DEET 137
Demodex mite **137**
Demodicosis 136-137
Dental care 121, 123
Department of Molecular
  Human Genetics of Ruhr
  University 55

Desert type 15-16, 22, 72
Deutscher Sloughi Club 32
*Deutscher Windhundzucht
  und Rennverband* 32
Diet 90
Differences
—among sighthounds 31, 34,
  42, 44
—in breeds 21
Digging 48, 52, 92
Dipylidium caninum 140,
  142
Dirofilaria immitis 141, **142**,
  143
Discipline 108
Distemper 10, 126, 128
DNA 13
Dog-fight 108
Dominance 111
Down 106, 111
Down/stay 112
Du Simoun Sloughis 22
Durel 9, 18
Durel, Pierre 22
Dutch Club for Oriental
  Sighthounds 28
Dutch Sloeqi Club 27-28
Ear
—care 95
—carriage 63
—cropping 18
—infections 57
—mites 135-136
Echinococcus multilocularis
  141
Egypt 10
Engelhardt, Mrs. 32
England 41
Escaping 52, 92
Estrus 128
Europe 19, 116-117
Exercise 50, 92
—pen 102
Expenses of ownership 81
External parasites 130-137
Eye problems 53
Family meeting the puppy
  86
Fear 89
Fédération Cynologique
  Internationale 15, 23, 58,
  144, 146
Feeding 90
Fenced yard 85, 92, 108
Field abilities 22
Finland 33
—milestones 36
First night in new home 87
Fleas **130**, 131, **132**
Food 90, 103
—bowls 78
—natural 90
Foundation Stock Service
  39

France 9-10, 19, 21, 117
—first breed standard 23
—milestones 25
French *Club du Sloughi* 23
Gait **65**, **70**
Gastric torsion 91
Genetic testing 119
Genotyping for PRA 55
Germany 10, 30, 55
—milestones 32
Golden-West kennel 36
Great Britain 42, 47, 144
—milestones 43
Greyhound
—compared to Sloughi **31**
Grooming 92
Guarding 46
Gum disease 121
Handling 147
Harper's magazine 39
Health 85
—adult 121
—concerns 53
—insurance for pets 125
—journal 86
—puppy 85, 119
—senior dog 123
Hearing 47, 55
Heart disease 123
Heartworm 121, 141, **142**,
  143
Heat cycle 128
Heel 114-115
Hepatitis 126, 128
Herding 117
Hereditary diseases 53
Heterodoxus spiniger **136**
Holland 10, 19, 24, 26
—milestones 28
Homemade toys 83
Hookworm **139**, **142**
Hormones 100
Hot weather 48
House-training 78, 91, 101-
  108
Hunting ability 9, 22, 46
Hunting events 116
Hypothyroidism 57
Immig, Mr. 28
Immune deficiencies 57
Independence 49
Infectious diseases 126
Instincts 48
Insurance 74, 125
Intelligence 49
Internal parasites 138-143
International All Breeds
  Canine Association 41
Ixodes dammini **133-134**
Judge 147
Jumping 52, 92, 106
Jutz, Mr. 32
Kennel Club, The 43, 58, 1
  146

Kidney problems 123
Kindergarten training 110
Large Gazehound Racing
    Association 38-39, 155
Lauer, P. 30
Le Gras, Auguste 9-10, 16,
    22, 26, 28
Leash 84, 102, 109
—pulling on 115
Leave it 108
Leishmania 10
Leliman, Mr. 24, 28
Leptospirosis 126, 128
Lewis, Jack William 38
Libya 9, 11, 15, 17-18
Lifespan 53, 73, 123
Louse **136**
Loyalty 49, 73
Lure coursing 38, 147, 154
Lyme disease 128
Mammary cancer 128
Mauvy, Robert 22
McGuffin, Jack 38-39
Mégnin, Pierre 9
Mites **135**, 136, **137**
Montouchet de la Horde
    d'Or 24
Moreau-Sipiere, Mrs. 38
Morocco 9-11, 15, 18, 23
Mosquitoes 137, 141 143
Mountain type 15-16, 22,
    72
Mounting 128
Multi-dog household 92
Nail trimming 94
Name 110, 114
National Open Field
    Coursing Association 39
National Oval Track Racing
    Association 38, 155
Neutering 85, 121, 128-129
Nomadic tribes 9
Non-core vaccines 128
North Africa 9-11, 15, 46
—traditions in 17
North American Coursing
    Association 39
Nubia Memorial Cup 39
Obedience 112, 117, 148
—classes 100, 115
—trials 115, 148
Off 106
Okay 112, 115
Open field hunts 116-117
OptiGen 41, 55
Origin
—countries of 11, 15-17, 21
—of breed 10-11
Other dogs 50, 92, 128
Otodectes cynotis 135
Ottoman Empire 12
Ouled-Nails kennel 32
Outdoor safety 85
Ovariohysterectomy 128
Ownership 74-75
—expenses of 81
Pain 52
Paper-training 101, 106
Parainfluenza 128

Parasites
—control 121
—external 130-137
—internal 138-143
Parvovirus 10, 126, 128
Personality 46, 49
Plants 84
Playtime 113
Poisons 84-85, 91
Porvali, Aili 36
Positive reinforcement 87,
    101, 108, 110
PRA 41, 53
Practicing commands 111-112
Praise 101, 108
Preventative care 119, 123
Proglottid **141**
Progressive retinal atrophy
    41, 53
Prostate problems 128
Protective instinct 49
Prussia, Princes August
    Wilhelm and Alexander
    Ferdinand of 30
Przezdziecki, Xavier 16, 22,
    24
Pulling on leash 115
Punishment 108-109
Puppy
—diet 90
—exercise 92
—first night in new home 87
—health 73, 85, 119
—kindergarten training class
    110
—meeting the family 86
—needs 101
—newborn 72
—personality 74, 121
—selection 72-74, 119
—socialization 88
—training 89, 100
Puppy-proofing 84-85
Rabies 10, 86, 126, 128
Racing 23, 32-33, 38, 116, 148,
    155
Rare Breed Kennel Club 38
Rawhide 81
Rechzaid, Mario 38
Reward 108
Rey, Agnes 24
Rhabditis **142**
Rhodesian Ridgeback **14,** 15
Roaming 46, 128
Rodarty, Kate and Carl 37
Romans 11
Rope toys 81
Ruspoli, Princess 15
Safety 79, 84, 91, 92, 102,
    104, 108, 113
—commands 108
—in the car 108
    outdoors 85
Sahara 9, 12, 16
Saluki 13, **19**, 21, 43
—compared to Sloughi **34,**
    35, 43, **45**
Sarcoptes scabiei 135

Scabies 135
Scenting 47, 55
—ability 117
—attraction 107
Schedule 107
Schmid, Armin 18
Schritt, Mr. and Mrs. 28
Schuru-esch-Schams kennel
    25, 28, 30
Second Punic War 11
Senior dog 90, 123
Senses 47, 55
Sensitive nature 101
Sensitivity to anesthesia 53,
    86, 123
Sheik el Arab kennel 30
Shi'Rayân Sloughis 38, 41
Show potential 144
Shyness 49, 73
Sigaux, Mrs. 23
Sighthound
—African 15
—ancient 10, 13
—differences among 21, 31,
    34, 42, 44
—events 116
Sit 110
Sit/stay 112
Size 17
Skin problems 129
SLAG 23
Sloughi Club (of UK) 43, 146
Sloughi Fanciers Association
    of America 38, 41, 55, 144
Sloughis d'Ymauville 23
Sloughis des Barines 23
Slughi 13
Socialization 48-49, 73, 88-
    89, 110, 121
Soft toys 81
Spaying 85, 121, 128
Specialty shows 146
—first 39
Sprint racing 117
St. Louis Area Sighthound
    club 39
Stacul, Mrs. F. 23
Standard 58, 144
—United Kennel Club 58
States Kennel Club 39, 41
Stay 112, 115
Supervision 106
Surgery 129
Sweden 36
Swiss Club for the Sloughi
    and the Azawakh 33
Switzerland 32, 33
Taenia pisiformis **141**
Tapeworm 140, **141, 142**
Teeth 121
Temperament 9, 46, 49
—evaluation 121
Temperature 124
Testicular cancer 128
Therapy work 117
Tick-borne diseases 133
Ticks **133-134**
Timing 107, 113
Touareg 19

Toxascaris leonine 138
Toxins 84-85
Toxocara canis **138**
Toys 80, 103-104
Tracking 117, 148, 150
Traditions 17
Training 50
—adult 100
—basic commands 110-115
—crate 101-108
—for special events 116
—importance of timing 107,
    113
—puppy 89, 100
Travel 104
Traveling 79, 108
Treats 87, 108
Trichuris sp. **140**
Tunisia 9, 11, 15-16, 18
Type
—desert 15-16, 22, 72
—mountain 15-16, 22, 72
United Kennel Club 41, 58,
    144, 146
—breed standard 58
United States 116-117
—milestones in racing 40
—milestones in show ring 40
—stud books in 41
United States Dog Agility
    Association 148
Urine marking 128
US 116-117
Vaccinations 85-86, 89, 121,
    126
—core vs. non-core 128
—issues regarding proper
    protocol 127
Van Duyvenbode, Mrs.
    Heather 17, 37, 28
Vandals 11, 13
Versatility 117
Veterinarian 81, 83, 85-86,
    108, 121
—selection of 123
Veterinary insurance 73, 125
Vision 47, 55
Visiting the litter 73-74
Wait 108
Waizenegger 9, 15
Walker, Mrs. Helen
    Whitehouse 148
War between France and
    Algeria 10, 19
Water 91, 103
—bowls 78
Weather 48, 52
West Nile virus 137
Whining 88, 104
Whipworm **140**
Windecker-Castan, Mrs. E.
With children 50, 87, 89
With other animals 50, 92 128
With strangers 49
Working breed 46
World Dog Show 32
Worm control 140
World War II 10, 23, 28, 30
Yard 85, 92, 108

My Sloughi

PUT YOUR PUPPY'S FIRST PICTURE HERE

Dog's Name _____

Date _____ Photographer _____